Cambridge Ele

Elements in the Philosophy ~~~~~
edited by
Grant Ramsey
KU Leuven
Michael Ruse
Florida State University

HYLOMORPHISM

William M. R. Simpson
*University of Texas at Austin and
University of Cambridge*

CAMBRIDGE
UNIVERSITY PRESS

CAMBRIDGE
UNIVERSITY PRESS

Shaftesbury Road, Cambridge CB2 8EA, United Kingdom

One Liberty Plaza, 20th Floor, New York, NY 10006, USA

477 Williamstown Road, Port Melbourne, VIC 3207, Australia

314–321, 3rd Floor, Plot 3, Splendor Forum, Jasola District Centre,
New Delhi – 110025, India

103 Penang Road, #05–06/07, Visioncrest Commercial, Singapore 238467

Cambridge University Press is part of Cambridge University Press & Assessment,
a department of the University of Cambridge.

We share the University's mission to contribute to society through the pursuit of
education, learning and research at the highest international levels of excellence.

www.cambridge.org
Information on this title: www.cambridge.org/9781009410830
DOI: 10.1017/9781009026475

First published 2023

A catalogue record for this publication is available from the British Library.

ISBN 978-1-009-41083-0 Hardback
ISBN 978-1-009-01284-3 Paperback
ISSN 2515-1126 (online)
ISSN 2515-1118 (print)

Hylomorphism

Elements in the Philosophy of Biology

DOI: 10.1017/9781009026475
First published online: May 2023

William M. R. Simpson
University of Texas at Austin and University of Cambridge

Author for correspondence: William M. R. Simpson, wmrs2@cam.ac.uk

Abstract: This Element introduces Aristotle's doctrine of hylomorphism, which provides an account of substances in terms of their 'matter' and 'form', adapting and applying it to the interface between physics and biology. It begins by indicating some reasons for the current revival of hylomorphism and by suggesting a way of classifying the confusing array of hylomorphisms that have arisen. It argues that, in order for composite entities to have irreducible causal powers which make a difference to how nature unfolds, they must have substantial forms which transform their matter such that the powers of their physical parts are grounded in the composite entity as a whole. It suggests how a contemporary form of hylomorphism might contribute to the philosophy of biology by grounding the non-intentional form of teleology that features in the identity conditions of biological systems, affirming a real distinction between living organisms and heaps of matter. This Element is also available as Open Access on Cambridge Core.

This Element also has a video abstract: www.cambridge.org/hylomorphism

Keywords: hylomorphism, causal powers, substantial forms, teleology, emergence

ISBNs: 9781009410830 (HB), 9781009012843 (PB), 9781009026475 (OC)
ISSNs: 2515-1126 (online), 2515-1118 (print)

Contents

1 The Fall and Rise of Hylomorphism

Holism, broadly speaking, is the view that the properties of the parts of a whole depend on the nature and existence of the whole. Holism is in vogue in the philosophy of science and receives a more receptive ear among metaphysicans today than it did in the early days of analytic philosophy: biological organisms are often touted as paradigmatic examples of irreducible wholes, in which the parts of an organism are 'caught up in a life' such that they compose some-thing novel and unified.[1] Yet how can a whole be 'more than the sum of its parts',[2] such that the whole is irreducible to the properties of and relations between them? Alternatively, how could the parts of a composite be related to one another in such a way that they compose a unified whole?

These questions have a special relevance for the philosophy of biology in relating the kinds of entities studied by biologists to the kinds of entities inves-tigated by physicists. Are biological organisms just arrangements of physical entities picked out by our best physics, which we happen to count as individ-uals, or is there something about the *nature* of an organism which demands that it should be counted as an individual in its own right? In this section, I shall out-line Aristotle's doctrine of hylomorphism, which explains the nature and unity of a biological whole in terms of its having a 'form' as well as matter. I will consider why this doctrine was abandoned by early modern philosophers in the wake of the Scientific Revolution, and why contemporary metaphysicians and philosophers of science are discussing it once again.

How Is Change Possible?   For much of the high scholasticism of the Middle Ages, prior to the Scientific Revolution, the philosophy of nature was con-cerned with placing common conceptions of experience within a more abstract but broadly realist philosophical framework derived from the metaphysics of Aristotle; a philosophy intended to interpret the world of ordinary experience rather than shatter it. Although medieval philosophers disagreed about many of the details of their metaphysical systems, and interpreted Aristotle in a wide variety of different ways, they were united in believing the world to be made up of 'substances', which are individuals that are irreducible to more basic constituents, and which are said to act in the world according to their own 'natures'.[3]

---

[1] The phrase was introduced by the philosopher Peter van Inwagen (van Inwagen, 1995), adapted from the biologist J. Z. Young's phrase, 'caught up into the living system' (Young, 1971).

[2] The phrase is often attributed to Aristotle. Significantly, however, Aristotle describes the whole as being something besides the parts (see *Metaphysics* VIII.6,1045a. 8–10.).

[3] This vision of nature also provided a basis for a natural law theory of ethics (Angier, 2021).

Whereas Plato conceived substances to be eternal and immaterial kinds that characterise the ephemeral things of nature, Aristotle maintained that substances exist as mutable parts of the natural world. According to Aristotle, properties may be predicated of a substance, some of which are essential to being a substance of that kind, but a substance is not itself predicable of anything else. His paradigm examples of substances are *living beings*, which maintain their complex identities through change. Pasnau has identified four 'common sense' assumptions of the Aristotelian-Medieval worldview (Pasnau, 2011, p. 633), which were challenged by the philosophy of nature that ultimately displaced it:

(A_1) We can have knowledge of the substances that exist in the physical world and of the natural kinds to which they belong.

(A_2) A folk ontology based on ordinary experience can carve things up in the physical world according to their true natures.

(A_3) Many of the objects of ordinary experiences – trees, cats, people, and so on – are in fact real substances.

(A_4) Substances naturally come into and go out of existence.

The confidence in ordinary experience which characterises this vision of reality – and the faith it places in the powers of sensory perception to disclose the existence and properties of substances – finds its source in Aristotle's 'hylomorphic' account of the nature of substances. This metaphysical account was born from his struggle to overcome various kinds of scepticism that he encountered in the work of ancient philosophers, such as scepticism concerning the possibility of change or of the possible existence of a plurality of entities. An essential step in Aristotle's account of how change and multiplicity are possible was to posit a fundamental distinction between *actual* and *potential* being. This distinction offered a way of carving a via media between the teachings of the Eleatics, on the one hand, and those of the Heracliteans, on the other.

Parmenides of Elea is widely understood to have denied that change is a real feature of reality: there is real being, but no real *becoming*. For a change to take place in nature – that is, for something new to arise in reality – it could not have been real before it occurred, and this can only mean, according to Parmenides, that it must have arisen out of nothing. Yet the event of something arising from nothing is inexplicable and an offence against reason (at least, for ancient philosophers). In the second part of his poem, *On Nature*, Parmenides can be construed as taking the following line of argument: if real change is possible, being must arise from non-being. However, being (something) cannot possibly arise out of non-being (nothing). Therefore, real change is impossible.

Parmenides denied the possibility of multiple beings on similar grounds: there can be unity but no multiplicity. For there to be real multiplicity, it would have to be the case that one part of reality *lacks* what another part has, and thus non-being would have to be the cause or source of their multiplicity.[4] Yet even if nothing (non-being) is an intelligible metaphysical concept, it does not refer to anything that exists, and cannot therefore be used to mark where one being begins and another ends. To put the argument more succinctly: if real multiplicity is possible, one being must be distinguished in reality from another being by non-being (nothing). However, one being cannot possibly be distinguished in reality from another being by non-being (nothing). Therefore, real multiplicity is impossible. For Parmenides, reality is fundamentally One and any changes that we perceive are only appearances.

The Heracliteans, on the other hand, are portrayed by Aristotle as taking the opposite view to Parmenides (in Metaphysics IV.5, at 1010a10 and following): the world is always changing, and it is our impressions of unity and persistence, rather than our impressions of change and multiplicity, which pertain to appearance rather than reality. In the limiting case, reality is a flux of multiplicity in which nothing in nature persists in the relentless succession of events.

Both of these sceptical extremes do violence to ordinary experience and give rise to performative self-contradictions: the reality of change and multiplicity is presupposed, for example, in the attempt of one person to persuade another to adopt Parmenides' views by articulating the steps of his argument. Likewise, the reality of unity and persistence is presupposed by a philosopher who professes unwavering fidelity to the sort of sceptical views that Aristotle attributed to the Heracliteans. Seeking to avoid such absurdity, Aristotle theorised that some beings are composites of both actual and potential being, introducing the concept of *potentiality* (or being-in-potency) as a middle ground between non-being and *actuality* (or being-in-activity).

Utilising the concept of potentiality, Aristotle was able to solve Parmenides' puzzles by denying the first premise in both the aforementioned arguments: change does not involve being arising from non-being, in contradiction of the immemorial principle, *ex nihilo nihil fit*;[5] rather, the transition is from being-in-potency to being-in-activity. This occurs when something exercises a *power* according to its nature. For example, a philosopher who, by exercising their intellectual powers, becomes convinced by Parmenides' arguments

---

[4] Or, to impose a more modern parlance about Parmenides' discussion: for two beings to be distinct in reality – that is, not merely in our conceptual schemes – there must be some property which one has but the other lacks, and this can only mean, according to Parmenides, that the difference between them must be grounded in the lack of something, which is literally, *nothing*.

[5] That is, *nothing comes from nothing*; a philosophical dictum put forward by Parmenides.

changes from being potentially Parmenidean to being an active disciple. Likewise, non-being is not the only principle by means of which two beings might be differentiated: two things can be differentiated by reference to their potentialities. Someone who is an *actual* disciple of Parmenides, for instance, differs from someone who is *potentially* Parmenidean but does not exercise their mind about such questions.

By distinguishing actual from potential being, Aristotle was also able to troubleshoot the counterintuitive view of change he attributed to the Heraclitians. After all, it is difficult to make sense of change without the concept of an actual state towards which change is moving (or from which it is departing). There also seems to be a need for some persisting actuality which can serve as the subject or underlying substrate of that change. Our scientific inquiries inevitably invoke the concept of actuality, as well as potentiality, when they pose the questions '*what* is changing in this physical system?' and 'in what *ways* can it change?'

Aristotle's distinction between actuality and potentiality thus opened a conceptual space for a philosophical account of ordinary experience which steers between the Heraclitian and Parmenidean rocks of scepticism: one which affirms the reality of change and multiplicity by endowing things in nature with powers. Nonetheless, even if change and multiplicity are admitted as part of reality, there is an important distinction between the kinds of changes that things undergo that was also subject to scepticism among ancient philosophers. On the one hand, there is the kind of change which involves the alteration of something, as when a scholar gains knowledge (an accidental change). On the other hand, there is the kind of change which involves the corruption of one thing and the generation of another, as when a Nordic warrior dies in fierce battle and a delicate flower springs up from the burial mound (a substantial change).

According to the philosopher Democritus and his teacher Leucippus, things only appear to go into and out of existence. We should account for the reality of all change in terms of the alteration of small, indivisible bodies (metaphysical atoms) of which everything else is composed. Contrary to Parmenides, Democritus argued that change does not require something to come into being out of nothing, but rather the existence of some persisting material principles that are continually rearranging themselves within an infinite void to form the changing world of appearances. Biological entities, such as cats and dogs, are not part of nature's ontology; in reality, there are just the metaphysical atoms, some of which may happen to be arranged cat-wise or dog-wise.

Aristotle's concepts of matter (*hyle*) and form (*morphe*) opened conceptual space for a realist account of substantial and accidental change as distinct kinds of change that occur in nature (see Aristotle, *Physics* I.7–9). His conception of matter differs significantly from that of Democritus. For Aristotle, matter is that which gets actualised or determined, whereas form is that which actualises or determines matter; the two metaphysical principles are essential to the being of all sensible substances and they cannot be physically separated. Both matter (which is the principle of potential being) and form (which is the principle of actual being) are required to explain the changes we observe in nature, along with the concept of privation, which is the lack of the form that is required by whatever the *telos* (end) of the change happens to be.

For instance, when an animal consumes a plant, the animal (a substance) is a subject of accidental change: by exercising its powers of digestion, the animal gains muscular mass it was previously lacking, yet remains the same animal. The matter of the animal – sometimes called 'secondary matter' – is thus said to have the potential to be actualised by different *accidental forms*. But this is not the only kind of change taking place. By being transformed into the flesh of the animal, the matter of the plant is stripped of the substantial form and those powers that are essential to being that kind of plant, and acquires the substantial form and those powers that are essential to being that kind of animal. The matter underlying these substances, which was understood by many medieval philosophers to be a wholly metaphysical 'prime matter', is thus said to have the potential to be actualised by different *substantial forms*.[6] It is because substances are composites of matter and form that they can be *subjects* of change, having both a determinate nature and a potential to be actualised.

Much is supposed to rest, then, upon the concept of substantial form for making sense of our ordinary experience of change. Indeed, the concept of substantial form has been widely considered by philosophers to play all of the following explanatory roles in the Aristotelian-Medieval account of substances:[7]

(R_1) Substantial form determines the kind of substance a thing is by determining its (essential) properties and causal powers.
(R_2) Substantial form determines those sensible qualities our folk ontologies rely upon for carving nature into different substances.

---

[6] It is controversial among ancient philosophers whether Aristotle requires the concept of prime matter in his account of hylomorphism. Scholars agree that for Aristotle, the matter underlying animals is something like flesh, bone, or blood. They also agree, however, that *if* prime matter arises in Aristotle, it properly arises in the context of the generation of the four elements.

[7] Picked out and indexed according to the common-sense theses (A_1–A_4) identified by Pasnau (2011). I do not say that they are necessary and sufficient conditions for being a substantial form.

(R_3) Substantial form is the principle of unity which explains the existence of composite entities that count as individual substances.

(R_4) Substantial form grounds the natural distinction between substantial change (generation and corruption) and accidental change.

The first role of substantial form (R_1) supports the first of the four common-sense assumptions of the Aristotelian-Medieval worldview (A_1): we have the prospect of becoming acquainted with the nature of a substance by discerning its powers, since different kinds of substances have different kinds of powers. The second role of substantial form (R_2) supports the second common-sense assumption which came into dispute (A_2): at least some substances can be discerned in ordinary experience in virtue of their sensible qualities. Likewise, the third role of substantial form (R_3) supports the third assumption (A_3): the domain of Aristotle's substances, unlike Democritus' atoms, is not confined to any particular physical scale – either the microscopic or the cosmic scales – but encompasses many of the middle-sized objects of ordinary experience, including biological entities such as plants and animals. Finally, its fourth role (R_4) supports the fourth assumption (A_4): when one thing comes into being and another is corrupted, this is not merely the alteration of something more fundamental, such as Democritus' atoms, but due to the action of substantial forms in transforming matter to generate a new fundamental reality.

Why Did Hylomorphism Fall into Disrepute?   Whether Aristotle's doctrine of hylomorphism, as it was originally formulated or subsequently interpreted, succeeded in supporting theses (A_1) to (A_4) is a matter for contentious debate. The cursory description that I have given only touches the bare bones of a doctrine that raises many metaphysical questions, and which was interpreted in a variety of ways within the medieval tradition.[8]

On the one hand, it was widely agreed that Aristotelian substances are supposed to have a *per se unity* which other kinds of entities lack. An aggregate entity, such as a pile of bricks or a heap of sand, is composed of physical parts which can exist independently of the wholes of which they are parts, and which retain their natures and identities even whilst they are composing the aggregate. An aggregate entity thus derives its being from the sum of its actual parts. In contrast, a living substance, such as a whale or a horse, is an irreducible whole whose organs are supposed to depend for their natures and identities upon the substance as a whole. Many Aristotelians have understood his notion of substance to imply that all of the *physical parts* of a substance (if it may be said

---

[8] A few paragraphs of this subsection draw verbatim on my discussion in Simpson (2018).

to have 'parts') are also supposed to depend for their natures and identities upon the substance as a whole. Although a living substance such as a horse is corrupted into a collection of non-living chemicals when it dies, which do not depend upon the original substance for their existence, these entities are not *numerically identical* to any parts of the substance that existed prior to its corruption. The substances into which a substance may be corrupted are typically said by Aristotelians to exist only *in potential* – or, as 'potential parts' rather than 'actual parts' – just so long as the substance itself continues to exist.[9]

Yet how should we understand the nature of matter and form in Aristotle's hylomorphic analysis of substance? Are they some kind of metaphysical parts which fit together to compose a physical substance, or are they merely conceptually useful ways of analysing entities which may be mereologically simple? If a substance is endowed with parts, how is its substantial form supposed to unify them to compose something which is metaphysically one?

Whilst many modern readers of Aristotle regard his theory of hylomorphism as a useful way of thinking about substances, but do not believe the concepts of matter and form are supposed to carve nature at the joints, philosophers within the scholastic tradition generally conceived matter and form as metaphysical constituents, believing that they are real and contribute to the whole. According to Aquinas, the unity of a substance that is metaphysically composed of matter and form pertains to its having a *single* substantial form which, whilst having no powers to influence directly the behaviour of other substances, explains the nature and unity of the physical substance which it in-forms by determining the properties of its matter and fixing its powers. Although matter and form cannot be separated *physically* from one another, they are metaphysical realities which can be separated *conceptually* through an intellectual process of abstraction.

The subsequent trajectory of hylomorphic metaphysics in the Middle Ages, however, has been characterised as one of an increasing fragmentation of the unity of substance and physicalisation of the concept of matter (Pasnau, 2011). For instance, Aquinas's characterisation of matter as a substrate of *pure potentiality*, which lacks any properties apart from form, was widely criticised by other scholastics for failing to bottom out in anything concrete or determinate which could serve as an intelligible substrate of substantial change, and was never widely accepted. Duns Scotus insisted against Aquinas that matter should have actual parts.[10] William of Ockham, writing in the early fourteenth century, went so far as to say that substances must be composed of actual substances.[11]

---

[9] See Aristotle, *de Generatione et Corruptione* I.10, and Aristotle, *Metaphysics* VII.

[10] See Scotus (Rep. II.12.2 n. 7 (XI:322b) in Wolter and Bychkov (2004).

[11] For a discussion of Ockham's view, see Pasnau (2011), 'Matter and extension'.

Likewise, the 'unitarian' doctrine of substantial form that Aquinas advocated (Wippel, 2000, pp. 327–51), in which a substance is attributed a single substantial form that determines all of its essential causal powers, was widely rejected by other scholastics.[12] According to Scotus, the form of *corporeity* (by which an animal is embodied) and the form of the *soul* (by which an animal is living) are present simultaneously within a human substance. Others embraced more extreme degrees of pluralism. As Zabarella remarked: 'if two forms at once are not contrary to reason, then neither will it be contrary for there to be four or a hundred at once in the same substance'.[13] Yet if multiple substantial forms can exist within the same substance, and if the matter of this substance is composed of actual parts which have their properties and identities independently of its substantial form, wherein lies the unity of the substance?

The mechanical philosophy of the seventeenth century that rapidly replaced the hylomorphic metaphysics of the scholastics, far from arising out of a philosophical vacuum, represents a development in these tendencies within medieval philosophy, which culminated in the physicalisation of matter as a substrate of actual parts and the rejection of any role for substantial form, such as its role of determining the properties of matter (R_1). The corpuscularianists proposed a much simpler ontology consisting of corpuscles arranged within physical space which have intrinsic and determinate properties, echoing the atomism of Leucippus and Democritus that Aristotle had so vehemently opposed.

In doing so, corpuscularianists were seeking to place their metaphysics in service to a new physics, which promised greater power over nature than Aristotle's physics, and to wrest the philosophy of nature from the metaphysical wranglings of the scholastics, which they perceived to be endless and exasperating.[14] In the old vision of nature which had dominated the Middle Ages, substances were reckoned to have metaphysical constituents which could be discerned through a process of intellectual abstraction. In the new vision of nature fomented by the Scientific Revolution, however, nature's building blocks are disclosed only to scientists who have been technically trained to measure and manipulate them.

---

[12] William de la Mare attacked Aquinas' affirmation of unicity in *Correctorium Fratris Thomae*.

[13] *De rebus naturalibus*, De gen. ch. 2, cols. 397–7, as translated in Pasnau (2011).

[14] There were also theological motivations for abandoning the medieval synthesis in favour of a mechanical, corpuscularian conception of nature, which I have not the space to discuss here: the rise of a voluntarist conception of God (Gillespie, 2008); a desire for a more modest metaphysics in the light of God's arbitrary power (Olson, 2004); a concern to address superstition by securing a clean separation between the natural and the supernatural (Olson, 2004); and a revived concern with apparent contradictions between the teachings of Aristotle and Christian doctrines concerning creation and the soul (Funkestein, 1986). The rise of Protestantism in Europe contributed to the decline of the medieval synthesis in multiple ways (Gregory, 2015).

The corpuscularian philosophy of nature swiftly supplanted scholasticism in many parts of Europe, as scientists like Robert Boyle contrived plausible mechanical explanations for natural phenomena, specifically targeting cases in physics where scholastics had attributed phenomena to the activities of forms.[15] Henry Oldenburg, who served as the first secretary for the Royal Society, memorably complimented Boyle for having 'driven out that drivel of substantial forms' which 'has stopped the progress of true philosophy, and made the best of scholars not more knowing as to the nature of particular bodies than the meanest ploughmen'.[16] Whilst corpuscularianists maintained a commitment to the notion of a material substrate underlying all change – in Boyle's view, a 'substance extended, divisible, and impenetrable'[17] – the doctrine of substantial forms was swiftly abandoned during the course of the seventeenth century (albeit with some notable dissenters, such as Leibniz).

The extirpation of form was accompanied by a lapse into a Democritean account of generation and corruption. According to Boyle, the material world laid bare by the physical sciences is a 'contrivance of brute matter managed by certain laws of local motion' (Boyle, 2000, vol.10, p. 447). Without immanent forms to explain things' powers, natural philosophers invoked extrinsically imposed laws to explain the motions of microscopic corpuscles and how things come into and go out of existence in the macroscopic world of appearances (Silva, 2019, p. 64–5). Substantial change was consigned once again to the world of appearances, since the material corpuscules of which everything is made persist through time and only change with respect to accidents like position.

In summary, the rejection of hylomorphism can be attributed at least in part to a shift in the sympathies of philosophers back towards atomism in the wake of the development of modern science. The rise of corpuscularianism witnessed the reduction of the causal powers and sensible qualities of substances to the mechanical properties of matter (providing defeaters for assumptions (A_1) and (A_2)), as well as the elimination of metaphysical constituents and the rejection of Aristotle's concept of potentiality (providing defeaters for assumptions (A_3) and (A_4)). Likewise, the methodological monism associated with the new physics, which was supposed to uncover the microphysical laws governing the corpuscles, displaced confidence in the sensory powers of ordinary experience to discern macroscopic substances (providing defeaters for assumptions (A_2)

---

[15] See R. Boyle, The Origin of Forms and Qualities. In (eds.). m. Hunter and E. Davis, *The Works of Robert Boyle*, (London: Pickering & Chatto, 1999–2000).

[16] H. Oldenburg, *Correspondence*, ed. and trans., A. R. Hall and M. B. Hall (Madison: University of Wisconsin Press, 1965), III:67.

[17] See Works of Boyle, V:305.

and (A_3)). Taken together, these changes conspired to call into question the nature of matter and the metaphysical roles of substantial form (R_1–R_4), driving a wedge between what Wilfrid Sellars famously called the 'scientific image' of reality – which is a view of reality that is based upon scientific inquiry – and the 'manifest image' of ordinary experience – which is a view of reality that is founded upon reflection on ordinary experience (Sellars, 1997).

Why Is Hylomorphism Making a Comeback?   Perhaps surprisingly, given its rather ignominious downfall, hylomorphism has been making a comeback in contemporary philosophy, with many prominent and up-and-coming philosophers identifying as hylomorphists of one form or another, including Kit Fine, Kathrin Koslicki, Mark Johnston, Alexander Pruss, Robert Koons, Anna Marmodoro, David Oderberg, Michael Rea, William Jaworski, and many others besides.[18] Yet, why should modern philosophers be interested in retrieving hylomorphism from the intellectual dustbin of history?

Corpuscularianism, which is the philosophical ancestor of the physicalism that held sway over the analytic philosophy of the last century, had a delicate balancing act to perform between two impulses that push in opposite directions. On the one hand, there is the desire to prune ontology down to nothing but the referents of our 'best physics' for simplicity's sake. On the other hand, there is a need to admit within one's ontology sufficient grounds for the sensory and cognitive powers upon which the scientific investigation of nature depends. The ontology of nature should be sparse, but not too sparse; otherwise, we risk being unable to cash out any of the truth claims of our best physics. The manifest image may be thrown into doubt, but not too much doubt; otherwise, we risk sawing off the epistemic branch upon which the physical sciences are sitting. There are good reasons to question, however, whether corpuscularianists or modern-day physicalists have succeeded in striking this delicate balance. Hence, there are good reasons to question the defeaters they generated against the four 'common-sense' assumptions of the Aristotelian-Medieval worldview (A_1–A_4).

In the first place, there has been a rise in 'neo-Aristotelian' metaphysics among contemporary analytic philosophers, which has included a return to essentialism, a restoration of substances, and the revival of Aristotle's doctrine of potentiality. Although the highly influential philosopher W. V. Quine had insisted that Aristotle's distinction between essence and accident is 'surely

---

[18] This renewed interest in hylomorphism reflects a broader interest in retrieving elements of Aristotle's metaphysics. See for example Simpson, Koons, and Teh (2017); and Simpson, Koons, and Orr (2021).

indefensible' for us today (Quine, 1960, p. 199), the concept of essence was subsequently reintroduced into analytic philosophy by Saul Kripke in the 1980s and given a robust logical foundation (Kripke, 1981). More recently, Kit Fine has argued that some things in nature are more fundamental than others (Fine, 2012), opening conceptual space for a theory of substances in which the less fundamental things in nature may be said to be 'grounded' (Schaffer, 2009). And although Hume famously rejected the notion that things have 'powers' to bring about change as a mere projection of our tendency to associate events that just happen to follow in succession, the concept of causal powers was reintroduced within analytic philosophy by Harré and Madden (1973).[19]

If we have good reason to think that the scientific revolutionaries threw the metaphysical baby out with the bathwater when they rejected the metaphysics of Aristotle along with his antiquated physics, then we have good reason to question corpuscularian defeaters for the assumption that there are substances in nature, such as organisms, which fall into natural kinds according to their causal powers (A_1). Corpuscularianists collapsed the identity conditions of substances by reducing their causal powers to the mechanical properties of matter. If there are distinct substances which have essential powers, however, then there may be a role for substantial form to play in determining those powers (R_1). We will consider the metaphysics of hylomorphic substances in Section 2.

In the second place, there are the broken promises of reduction which call into question the ontological adequacy of physicalism. The phenomenon of heat, for example, has *not* been successfully reduced to corpuscular motion,[20] and there may be cases of 'strong' emergence in nature – according to physicists (Bishop & Ellis, 2020) as well as philosophers (Gillett, 2016; J. M. Wilson, 2021) – which involve fundamentally novel features, causal powers, forces, or laws that obtain at higher levels of compositional complexity. Likewise, the recasting of the secondary qualities of substances as the subjective 'qualia' of conscious experience merely shifted the problem of their reduction from the philosophy of nature to the philosophy of mind, where they have proven stubbornly resistant to assimilation within any broadly consensual physicalism (Chalmers, 1996; Koons & Bealer, 2010; Robinson, 2016).

If we have good reason for thinking that modern-day physicalists have bitten off more than they can chew in trying to reduce the macroscopic world to the

---

[19] It was advanced by Martin (1994), developed by Molnar (2006), and supports a non-Humean theory of causation by Mumford and Anjum (2011). Marmodoro links powers to the concept of potentiality (Marmodoro, 2014). On the return of powers, see Lagerlund, Hill, and Psillos (2021).

[20] Although this claim has been repeated *ad nauseum* by analytic philosophers, temperature is not identical to 'mean kinetic energy' (Vemulapalli & Byerly, 1999, pp. 28–32).

microscopic world, then we have good reason to question the corpuscularian defeaters for common-sense assumptions about the existence of macroscopic objects (A_3–A_4). The corpuscularianists sought to confine ontology to facts about the microscopic constituents which supposedly compose everything, reducing the objects of ordinary experience to mere collectives. If there are fundamental properties that obtain at higher levels of compositional complexity, however, there may be a role for something like substantial form to play in explaining the generation and persistence of entities that possess them (R_3–R_4). We will consider the emergence of higher-level powers in Section 3.

In the third place, the turn to practices in contemporary philosophy of science has called into question the epistemological foundations of corpuscularianism and modern-day physicalism. Nancy Cartwright has argued that successful sciences are those which measure things' causal powers (or 'capacities') rather than uncover universal laws of nature, embracing a methodological pluralism in which different practices are needed to uncover the various powers which things manifest in different contexts (Cartwright, 1999).[21] The turn to practices has been accompanied by the rapid development and expansion of philosophies of the specialised sciences, which assert the autonomy of the special sciences in relation to 'fundamental' physics. According to the philosopher of biology, Denis Walsh, for example, the view that material constitution alone determines the properties of complex entities 'gets in the way' of biology affirming what it ought to be able to affirm about 'the self-building, self-maintaining, processual, and emergent capacities' of organisms (Walsh & Wiebe, 2020, p. 108).

If we have good reason to think that physicalists have exaggerated the unity and universality of physics, then we have good reason to question corpuscularian defeaters for the assumption that there are some substances which can be discerned through ordinary experience (A_2). The corpuscularianists sought to impose a methodological monism in which physics is the only reliable way of finding out about fundamental reality. If there are emergent entities with real, irreducible features which can be picked out in other ways, however, then there may be a role for substantial form in determining those qualities and causal powers which are relevant to discerning them (R_2). We will consider the possibility of identifying biological substances in Section 4.

In short, the growing interest in hylomorphism among philosophers may be attributed to a loss of confidence in microphysical reductionism and a rekindled interest in Aristotle's metaphysics. The relevance of hylomorphism to the

---

[21] Owen has applied this line of thought to cognitive neuroscience and the measurement of consciousness in unresponsive brain-injured patients, with a view to assimilating consciousness within a non-physicalist, hylomorphic conception of nature (Owen, 2021).

philosophy of biology, I suggest, consists in the possibility of providing an alternative characterisation of the ontological relationship between physics and biology to the non-reductive physicalist's hackneyed appeal to supervenience; a characterisation which, unlike physicalism, does not 'prevent us from saying what a science of organisms ought to be able to say' (Walsh & Wiebe, 2020, p. 122). According to Walsh, the time is ripe for a 're-evaluation of the merits of hylomorphism for biology' (Walsh & Wiebe, 2020, p. 108). As we shall see, however, not all modern versions of hylomorphism have been created equal. And the metaphysical details matter.

2 Modern Hylomorphisms

A number of notable philosophical theories have recently been put forward under the banner of 'hylomorphism'. In this section, I will seek to classify them in order to select a subset that is relevant to the philosophy of biology, and will discuss a metaphysical challenge for any modern-day hylomorphism that attempts to provide an ontology of biological substances, namely: the challenge of explaining the *unity* of a material substance. I will then consider how three different rival theories of hylomorphism try to meet this challenge.

What Do Modern Hylomorphists Have in Common?   According to Walsh, organisms are not merely material things, but are 'processual things', exercising a capacity to 'build and maintain structures' that perpetuate their existence and identity through material change (Walsh & Wiebe, 2020, p. 109).[22] What unites contemporary hylomorphists is their concern with the question of how something which is constituted by – or has its origins in – a plurality of entities can count as a single entity in its own right, even as its matter undergoes change. Koons and Evnine have both suggested ways of grouping these theories which I shall rework into a more comprehensive taxonomy, before focussing on three accounts I would like to consider in more detail.

For Koons, modern theories of hylomorphism should be classified as *staunch* or *faint-hearted* according to whether or not they offer 'a real distinction between living organisms and heaps of matter, without recourse to dualism or vitalism' (Koons, 2014, p. 151). To be 'staunch', Koons argues, a hylomorphist should be committed to the existence of a substantial form as 'a power that is the cause of the generation (by fusion) and persistence of a composite whole through time' (Koons, 2014, p. 1). Likewise, Koons thinks staunch hylomorphists should be ontologically committed only to a *sparsity* of natural properties that carve nature at the joints, in order to rule out the possibility

---

[22] For recent work on the processual nature of organisms, see Nicholson and Dupré (2018).

of 'coincident substances' which share the same materials at the same time (Koons, 2014, p. 157). It is because 'faint-hearted' hylomorphisms lack one or more of these features, Koons contends, that they fail to deliver the robust distinction between substances and mere collectives that Aristotle's doctrine was intended to achieve. By failing to reintroduce into ontology something that can play the roles of the concept of substantial form (R_1–R_4), they fall prey to Bernard Williams' criticism that hylomorphism is just a 'polite form of materialism' (Williams, 2006, p. 225). We shall consider Koons's most recent version of hylomorphism in more detail presently, which has evolved somewhat since he developed this taxonomy.

An example of faint-hearted hylomorphism, in Koons's view, is Johnston's liberal schema for composite entities (Johnston, 2006), where 'each genuine kind of complex item will have associated with it a characteristic principle of unity' (Johnston, 2006, p. 653). According to Johnston, what it is for a complex item X to exist is for the parts $y_1, y_2, \ldots$, which constitute its matter, to stand together in some relation R, which constitutes its principle of unity (Johnston, 2006, p. 658). For example: 'What it is for this hydrochloric acid molecule to be is for this positive hydrogen ion and this negative chlorine ion to be bonded together' (Johnston, 2006, p. 658).

Koons complains that Johnston fails to limit his hylomorphism to the generation of natural substances and that consequently he must countenance many cases of coincident objects, 'one corresponding to each relation R that is realised by any plurality of objects' (Koons, 2014, p. 151). Such a theory may be able to capture many of the items of folk ontology, but it does not offer a robust distinction between organisms and heaps of matter, since it inflates our ontology by counting all sorts of gerrymandered collections as substances – for example, 'a whole consisting of your eyeglasses and Pluto' (Johnston, 2006, p. 697).

Koslicki receives a similar appraisal from Koons for taking form to be merely a structural arrangement of something's matter, yet Johnston's and Koslicki's conceptions of hylomorphism differ in significant ways. Whereas Johnston thinks, for example, that the parts of a 'spork' (which has the tines of a fork at one end and the bowl of a spoon at the other) can constitute a plurality of different substances (Johnston, 2006, p. 665–7), Koslicki thinks that a given collection of entities can compose at most one entity and requires the structure that unifies them to be literally a *part* of the substance (Koslicki, 2008, 2018a).[23]

---

[23] Treating form as a part leads to a regress problem, however, which I will consider presently.

It does not seem fair to lump Koslicki with the 'faint-hearted' (Koons, 2014, p. 156).[24] As Evnine observes: 'Koons misses the way in which Koslicki's view approaches his [own]... since he mistakenly says that Koslicki is committed to the existence of an entity "for every arrangement realised by any plurality of objects"' (Evnine, 2016, p. 52). In fact, Koslicki conceives form as specifying 'a range of structural requirements which must be satisfied by the material parts composing a matter-form compound' (Koslicki, 2018b, p. 352), thus restricting the kinds of arrangements that count as substances. Yet Koslicki's hylomorphism cannot qualify as 'staunch' either, according to Koons's criteria, since she does not admit an ontology of powers (Koons, 2014, p. 156).[25]

Evnine has proposed an alternative binary distinction between *powers-based* and *principle-based* hylomorphisms (Evnine, 2016). Powers-based hylomorphists like Koons, he claims, 'look to powers, or dispositions, to discharge some of the work assigned by Aristotle to his notion of form' (p. 10). Principle-based hylomorphisms, however, are not concerned with the metaphysics of powers, but are united in their conception of substances as complex objects 'involving both matter and either a principle, property, relation, function or structure', which the matter of the composite may be said to exemplify. As Evnine observes, since principle-based hylomorphists typically do not conceptualise form as being the *cause* of the substance being *what* it is, they 'tend to take artifacts and organisms as being on an ontological level' (p. 1).

Evnine offers Fine as an example of a principle-based hylomorphist. Fine's conception of hylomorphism is similar to Johnston's but has some differences: it involves a theory of both 'variable' and 'rigid embodiments'. For a variable embodiment such as 'a container that has different water as a part at different times' (Fine, 1999, p. 69) – that is, an object which is mereologically incontinent – we need a 'principle' that has a unique 'manifestation' at every moment of time, where each manifestation is a rigid embodiment. For a rigid embodiment such as a bunch of flowers (Fine, 1999, p. 65) – that is, an object which has timeless parts – we require some relation R (the form) that obtains among parts a, b, c (the matter), which exists just in case these objects stand together in that relation.

Fine's principle-based hylomorphism is highly profligate. It seems that any rule or function we can think of which could yield a unique rigid embodiment for each moment of some interval could count as a principle. For

---

[24] Additionally, Koons's teasing terminology does not make allowance for the other uses to which non-powerist theories of hylomorphism might be put, such as the metaphysics of artifacts.

[25] Yet Koslicki does not reject powers outright either. Her account might be supposed to maintain neutrality on this point, whereas Koons's account insists that powers are necessary.

Table 1 Hylomorphisms categorised according to whether they conceive forms as metaphysical constituents or concepts, and whether or not they have power ontologies

Comparison of hylomorphisms across two categories		
	Powerist ontology	**Non-powerist** ontology
Matter and form as **metaphysical constituents**	Robert Koons William Jaworski	Kathrin Koslicki
Matter and form as **metaphysical concepts**	Anna Marmodoro	Kit Fine Mark Johnston

Koons's powers-based hylomorphism, however, substantial forms are supposed to be *sparse* powers which are to be found *in reality* and not merely in our representations.

Yet there are some hylomorphists, such as Marmodoro, who do not fall neatly under Evnine's binary distinction between powers-based and principle-based hylomorphists. On the one hand, Marmodoro is clearly committed to a fundamental powers ontology, since she claims that what exists fundamentally are physical powers (Marmodoro, 2017). In this respect, Evnine is correct to classify Marmodoro as a powers-based hylomorphist. On the other hand, Marmodoro insists that matter and form are *not* powers but principles (Marmodoro, 2013), and denies that substantial form is the cause of a substance being *what* it is. By using the principles of matter and form to explain how scientists carve up the world of powers (Marmodoro, 2018), we are supposed to get the various substances investigated by the special sciences as a 'free lunch', so to speak. Yet, in Marmodoro's theory of hylomorphism, as we shall see, substantial forms have no existence apart from the conceptual activity of carving the world into substances according to our explanatory interests.

Instead of proposing another binary division, I wish to put forward a taxonomy that divides theories across two categories. Along the rows of Table 1, I shall distinguish between *concept-based* hylomorphisms, in which matter and form are regarded as metaphysical concepts we can or should use for carving the world into substances, and *constituent-based* hylomorphisms, in which matter and form are considered to be metaphysical constituents of a substance which contribute to its physical being. What divides constituent-based hylomorphists from concept-based hylomorphists is their belief that substances exhibit this internal ontological complexity independently of our conceptual activities. Across the columns, I shall distinguish between *powerist* hylomorphisms, which make use of a powers ontology to explain change, and *non-powerist* hylomorphisms, which either reject causal powers in favour of a Humean ontology or remain neutral concerning whether we should adopt Humean assumptions about change. According to this classification scheme, concept-based and constituent-based hylomorphists can come in both powerist and non-powerist varieties.

Using this classification scheme, we can locate modern theories of hylomorphism which would otherwise be misplaced using Koons's binary distinction between staunch and faint-hearted hylomorphisms, such as Koslicki's version of hylomorphism. Koslicki may not be 'staunch' but it is misleading to lump her with the 'faint-hearted'. Rather, she can be more usefully identified as a non-powerist, constituent-based hylomorphist, sharing some features of her account in common with Koons and other features in common with Johnston. Likewise, using this scheme, we can find a place for theories which might otherwise be sidelined by Evnine's binary distinction between powers-based and principle-based hylomorphisms, such as Marmodoro's hylomorphic account. Marmodoro's theory is not usefully classified by placing it in the same category as Koons's. Rather, Marmodoro may be better understood as a powerist, concept-based hylomorphist, sharing some features of her account in common with Koons and other features in common with Fine.

Having settled on an ecumenical classification of contemporary theories of hylomorphism, I wish to converge upon a few contenders which may have special relevance for the philosophy of biology. Like Koons, I am looking for hylomorphic accounts which offer a real distinction between living organisms and heaps of matter. As we have seen, non-powerist hylomorphisms – like Fine's and Johnston's – are not primarily concerned with what we find in nature: they do not distinguish in any robust way between natural substances and artifacts. This is not in itself a criticism of their different projects, however, and should not in my view disqualify them from being classified broadly as 'hylomorphic'. Nonetheless, since I am interested in pursuing a naturalistic approach to ontology, in which what individuals there are is at least partly a matter for the sciences to decide, I shall focus on powerist hylomorphic theories.

Are Forms Structures?   According to Lowe, the primary metaphysical problem facing any version of hylomorphism is 'the challenge of explaining how a new substance is brought into existence' when matter and form combine (Lowe, 2012, p. 236). The hylomorphist must 'justify the judgment that a new concrete object – an "addition of being" – really has been brought into existence, rather than some previously existing things merely being rearranged' (Lowe, 2012).

Table 2 Powerist hylomorphisms categorised according to whether they conceive forms as metaphysical constituents or principles, and whether or not they are transformative

Comparison of powerist hylomorphisms across two categories		
	Transformative	**Structural**
Matter and form as **metaphysical constituents**	Robert Koons	William Jaworski
Matter and form as **metaphysical concepts**	Anna Marmodoro	

Yet what kind (or degree) of unity should a hylomorphic theory be trying to achieve? Different contemporary theories of hylomorphism set the bar at different levels. In some cases, the hylomorphic unity pertains to some fundamental physical constituents being *related* in a non-trivial way, such that they count as physical wholes according to certain functional criteria. In other theories, the unification of the parts within the whole goes deeper, such that the parts are made to depend upon the whole or are even annihilated within it.

The distinction I seek to elaborate here is between *structural hylomorphisms*, which deliver physical wholes whose parts are said to have been 'structured' in such a way that they fulfil certain functional roles within the composite, and *transformative hylomorphisms*, which deliver substantial wholes in which the matter from which they are generated has been 'transformed' such that the physical parts of the substance ontologically depend upon the whole for their causal powers or physical identities (see Table 2). Significantly, in a structured whole, the physical parts of the emergent entity do not depend for their definition upon the whole, but have a nature and properties of their own. Why might some powerists prefer to think of form in terms of structure and to dispense with any deeper metaphysical story about the transformation of their parts?

In the first place, some analytic metaphysicians have objected to the logical grammar of Aristotle's original account of hylomorphism. According to Lowe, Aristotle thinks of matter and form as being able to combine into a single whole because he thinks of each on its own as being somehow *incomplete* – an explanation that Lowe finds perplexing, since he fails to see how two 'incomplete' entities are supposed to combine to make a new thing, or the motivation for saying that form 'combines' with anything at all (Lowe, 2012).

Lowe offers the example of a proton and an electron combining to form a hydrogen atom for consideration. 'The form does not, in any sense I can understand, "combine" with the proton and the electron as to constitute with them the atom', he complains. 'The only things that do any "combining" are the proton and the electron' (p. 237). What we have is a new kind of physical arrangement, according to Lowe, in which 'a new form is instantiated'. Nonetheless, he thinks that 'some types of "rearrangement" are ontologically more weighty than others' because they exhibit novel causal powers (p. 237).

Jaworski offers a version of structural hylomorphism that purports to 'describe the case of the hydrogen atom in more or less the same way as Lowe' (Jaworski, 2016, p. 331). In this theory, form is conceived as being identical to the 'structure' of a physical composite. Whereas Lowe would 'prefer to abandon the term "matter" altogether' (Lowe, 2012, p. 237), the structural hylomorphist retains a role for a material continuant that gets 'structured' when the new substance is generated. In this particular case, the matter consists of the proton and the electron which get structured within the atom. Structure is considered to bestow the ontological weight upon the composite that is needed for it to count as a new substance, by endowing it with novel causal powers over and above the powers of its matter. These novel powers are discovered and described within whatever scientific practice is concerned with studying that kind of entity.

In the second place, some philosophers today are tempted to think of form as a type of structure because they believe our best physics has shown us that everything is made of microscopic particles or fields which are governed by universal laws, and that there is no longer good reason for positing a more metaphysical conception of matter such as the scholastic doctrine of prime matter. Cian Dorr offers a three-part recipe for constructing metaphysical hypotheses that has been described as 'orthodoxy for post-Quinean metaphysics' (Button, 2013, p. 12): first, a fundamental ontology of physical constituents is to be stated; second, a fundamental ideology should be specified in order to describe them; and finally, some physical laws must be laid down which 'capture important general patterns' among them (Dorr, 2011, p. 139).

Jaworski's version of structural hylomorphism offers to make peace with this widespread conception of the relationship between physics and metaphysics, providing a way of thinking about matter and form that avoids coming to blows with the notion that our 'best physics' characterises 'the fundamental physical particles or stuffs' of which everything is made (Jaworski, 2016, p. 25). 'When [structural] hylomorphists look at the world, they see the same sea of matter and energy that physicalists do', he suggests amicably, 'but they see something more besides: scattered throughout it are tiny localized pockets of order or arrangement' (Jaworski, 2016). In Jaworski's opinion, we should think of form as a kind of structure which organises or relates parcels of determinate physical stuff.

The apparent advantages in doing so are twofold. On the one hand, by appealing to 'structure' as a fundamental explanatory principle, we can explain how a complex composite acquires causal powers which are not determined by the powers of its physical parts. There is more to the world than can be described by our best physics. On the other hand, since structure is a relational concept, the parts which are picked out by our best physics do not lose the intrinsic properties they (supposedly) possessed 'in the wild'. They do not cease, then, to be physical entities with their own intrinsic identities, when they are structured within a composite. 'The materials, after all, can exist without being caught up into the whole', given this physicalised conception of matter, and our best physics will continue to 'describe the matter and energy that flow through structured individuals' (Jaworski, 2016) according to the same universal laws.

Jaworski seeks to situate his notion of hylomorphic structure within the context of a two-category, substance-attribute ontology, which takes substances (or individuals) and their properties (including polyadic properties or relations) to be fundamental (Jaworski, 2016, p. 27). We should think of hylomorphic structures as properties, according to Jaworski, rather than as individuals or parts of individuals (Jaworski, 2016, p. 94). More precisely, they are 'relations between [individual] wholes and their parts' (Jaworski, 2016, p. 96; fn. 2). As a powerist, Jaworski takes natural properties to be powers, so structures must also be powers. More specifically, they are 'powers... to configure (or organise, order, or arrange) materials' (p. 94), producing composite individuals which have higher-level powers in addition to the powers of their parts. Nonetheless, there can be no difference in something's higher-level properties without a difference in its physical properties. 'Higher-level conditions supervene on lower-level conditions', Jaworski admits, yet he insists that they are not *determined* by them (Jaworski, 2016, p. 288).[26] Jaworski's concept of structure is clearly intended to fill the roles of substantial form identified in Aristotle's doctrine of hylomorphism (R_1–R_4).

Do Substances Lack Proper Parts?   Transformative hylomorphists are wary of the reasons that structuralists give for reconditioning Aristotle's concept of form as structure. What Lowe overlooks in his criticisms of the grammar of traditional hylomorphism, according to Marmodoro, is the *complementarity* of the two things that are said to be combined: 'complementary entities complete each other on account of what is achieved when they complement one

---

[26] I discuss this compromise between physicalists and hylomorphists further in Section 3.

another. For Aristotle, the wholesomeness of the achievement is what licenses the description of the contributing entities as incomplete' (Marmodoro, 2018, p. 61–2). Yet to understand how matter and form are supposed to complement one another in the composition of a physical substance, we need a *metaphysical* conception of both matter and form.

Let us begin with Marmodoro's account of the transformation that is supposed to distinguish substances from heaps. According to Marmodoro, thinking of matter and form as *parts* of a substance undermines the unity that is supposed to distinguish a substance from a mere aggregate (Marmodoro, 2013).[27] The problem of unity can be brought into focus by considering Aristotle's famous syllable regress (see *Metaphysics* VII.17,1041b.11–33). As Aristotle pointed out in this puzzle, a syllable like 'BA' is something over and above the letters 'B' and 'A' of which it is constituted. Merely adding another element 'X' to the collection, however, whether X is conceived as a monadic entity or some kind of relation, would not unify the letters into a single syllable. Rather, the syllable would then be composed of three elements 'BAX', which would themselves have to be unified. Likewise, the flesh of an organism, although generated from certain physical elements – for Aristotle, the elements of 'earth' and 'fire' – is not generated by adding another element. What we must add is the *unifying principle* that, in the one case, makes the letter to be a syllable, and in the other case, makes the physical elements to be living flesh.

According to Marmodoro, such a principle should not be conceived as another part of the composite, in order to avoid falling into Aristotle's syllable regress. What is needed is something of a different ontological standing than the physical elements it is supposed to unify into a single substance. A substantial form, in her view, must be a principle which *transforms* these elements by supplying them with new *identity criteria*, such that all of the parts of the substance become dependent upon the identity criteria of the substance as a whole. Once they have been stripped of their distinctness, the elements may be said to exist 'holistically' in the substance rather than 'separately' (Marmodoro, 2013, p. 15). Yet what exactly does this conception of a substance's parts amount to?

In the end, it seems the most straightforward way to understand Marmodoro's notion of transformation is to say that a substance lacks any proper parts,[28] because the components from which it is generated are effectively *annihilated* and replaced by an atomic whole which lacks proper parts.[29] Such a substance

---

[27] Marmodoro thinks that 'matter and form are holistically rather than mereologically composed' (Marmodoro, 2018, p. 60).

[28] 'Proper part' is the mereological term that best corresponds in its application to our ordinary use of the term 'part', in that an object's proper parts exclude the object itself.

[29] Koons calls this thesis 'Aristotelian Parts-Nihilism' (Koons, 2014, p. 161).

is not a composite since it lacks any ontological complexity. It must therefore be unified *simpliciter*. Yet how is this radical transformation supposed to occur, and how are we to understand references to a substance's 'parts' and their powers?

We might try to understand such references as referring to entities which have the *potential* for existing outside of the substance. A human substance may contain various chemical compounds as *potential* parts, for example, which have no *actual* existence as long as the substance is living and whole, but which are actualised at death when this substance is subject to corruption. Yet as Koons complains, such an account offers counterintuitive results when applied to various organic parts, such as his heart or his hands. According to Aristotle's Homonymy Principle, a hand cannot exist except as part of the body, and a severed hand is a 'hand' in name only.[30] If a man's hands and his heart cannot exist as potential parts, according to the Homonymy Principle, and if they cannot exist as actual parts, according to Marmodoro's conception of transformation, then the causal powers that we ordinarily attribute to a man's organic parts, such as the power of his heart to pump blood, will have to be borne directly by the man himself. In that case, the term 'heart' could only refer, counterintuitively, to the whole man 'qua pumper of blood' (Koons, 2014, p. 161).

This radical transformation, in which the parts of a substance are 're-identified' within the whole substance, is clearly missing from Jaworski's constituent-based hylomorphism, in which the form which is added to the matter merely organises or relates certain physical elements that retain their physical identities within the structured composite. It is also missing from Koslicki's constituent-based hylomorphism, in which an object's matter consists of parts which are themselves hylomorphic compounds. Whatever is generated by adding an element of 'form' or of 'structure' to such a composite cannot, in Marmodoro's view, be considered metaphysically one, since such an element merely augments the internal ontological complexity of the composite.

Yet what could effect such a transformation? Marmodoro favours a one-category trope ontology, in which the world consists of physical tropes of powerfulness,[31] such as mass, spin, and charge. If the fundamental building blocks are powers which have physical identities independently of any substance, then the transformation of those elements into unified substance seems more like a conjuring trick than an operation of nature. How are we to make sense of it? According to Marmodoro, we need to distinguish between two kinds of unity which she believes many hylomorphists, including Aristotle

---

[30] In Aristotle's original example, it is a severed finger. See *Metaphysics* VII.10,1035b.23–25.

[31] A view she has developed as a modern reading of Aristotle (Marmodoro, 2014, Ch. 1).

himself, have run together (Marmodoro, 2018). In the first place, there is what she calls the *physical* unity of an *object*. The fundamental building blocks of nature, which are power-tropes, must be 'united' in some way in order to constitute an object (Marmodoro, 2017). In the second place, there is what she calls the *metaphysical* unity of a *subject* – of something qualified by certain powers. Marmodoro thinks the generation of any subject that may be said to possess its own powers involves a conceptual activity in which these powers are 'unified'.

For example, an electron – according to Marmodoro – is comprised of a certain structure of powers, namely: the fundamental powers of mass, spin, and charge. She thinks the structure which unites these distinct powers must involve something more than the mere compresence of these powers. However, she claims that scientists *also* think of an electron as a unified entity, which bears each of these powers as its own properties. The 'oneness' that emerges from the transformation of these elements is the oneness of a subject which is characterised by its physical constituents (for example, charge) as its physical *qualifications* (for example, being charged). It is the electron *qua* subject, rather than the electron *qua* object, which may be said to exercise the power of charge. Significantly, she thinks this metaphysical unity is achieved through an act of *conceptual individuation*, in which the physical constituents of a structure of powers are 're-identified' according to our explanatory interests (Marmodoro, 2018). This operation, which causes them to lose their individuality within the whole, is something *we* perform upon a substance's constituents. Does Marmodoro's account offer a *real* distinction, then, between living organisms and heaps of matter?

On the one hand, Marmodoro delineates a robust criterion for the unity of substances. Indeed, the bar is set very high: for something to count as a substance, all of its parts must be transformed such that they are identified by the substantial form of the substance. In her view, a substance can only have *potential* parts, which are 'parts' that have no actual existence within the substance as a whole but are identified through a process of abstraction. This must be so in order to preserve the metaphysical unity of the substance.

On the other hand, by grounding the distinction between substances and heaps upon a conceptual act of individuation, she resorts to a Kantian dualism between subject and object, in which the metaphysical unity of a substance depends upon *us* rather than upon nature. The line between substance and artifact is blurred, since substances are what we make them. Marmodoro's hylomorphism thus only offers a partial implementation of the roles of substantial form that were identified in the previous section (R_1–R_4), and offers only partial support for the 'common sense' assumptions with which they are associated (A_1–A_4).

On the positive side, we can *know* substances because we make them (A_1), and many of the objects of ordinary experience – including organisms – count as substances (A_3). On the flip side, this means that folk ontologies fail to carve any joints within nature, so (A_2) comes out false. The reason for this is that, in Marmodoro's account, substantial form does not play the role of *causing* a substance to be *what* it is (R_1), but only *specifies* the causal powers which qualify it, and the distinction between substantial and accidental change is not a *natural* distinction (R_4), but is something that *we* impose upon nature. Since scientists are free to carve up spatiotemporal regions in whatever ways they find pragmatically expedient, there are no facts concerning what substances exist.

In one sense, Marmodoro's theory of hylomorphism levels the playing field between physics and biology in a way that is relevant to this discussion: macroscopic biological organisms, such as cats and dogs, get to be just as 'real' as microscopic physical entities, such as protons and electrons. That is to say, they are all substances that scientists *construct* out of power-tropes according to their explanatory interests. In another sense, however, Marmodoro sees physics as being more fundamental than biology, because physical theories are afforded the privilege of picking out the powers comprising the fundamental ontology from which every *thing* (qua subject) must be made. Primitive powers, unlike substances, exist independently of how inquiring agents take things to be.

How Can Unity and Complexity Be Reconciled?   Although Marmodoro seeks to restrict the transformation which could explain the unity of a substance to the provenance of her own concept-based hylomorphism, her objection to constituent-based hylomorphisms should not be applied *tout court*. Anne Peterson has observed that Marmodoro's account of hylomorphism contains unstated Quinean assumptions about the univocal nature of being and unity, whereas for Aristotle 'there is no such thing as just being or just unity; these terms are equivocal' (Peterson, 2018, p. 3). If there is no unity that is not 'unity under some category of being', then the only way to draw constituent-based hylomorphists into Aristotle's syllable regress is to 'undermine unity under the category of being at hand' (p. 6). In this case, the relevant category is that of *substance*, and hence Marmodoro's objection to constituent-based hylomorphisms reduces to the objection that a substance, if it is a unified entity, cannot have other substances as actual parts.

Can hylomorphists coherently admit the possibility of substances in which form is the *cause* of the substance being what it is, without sacrificing the transformation that explains how the parts of a substance compose a *unified* whole? What is needed, I suggest, is a conception of matter and form as metaphysical constituents in which both may be seen to have a different ontological standing to the substance which they compose, and whose 'joint achievement' is an individual whose causal powers are determined by its substantial form. Aristotle employs the distinction between potentiality (or being-in-potency) and actuality (or being-in-activity) to distinguish matter and form from substance: matter is only *potentiality* for substance, whereas form 'is related to a substance as the *actuality* of that substance – its essence, or that which makes it what it is' (Peterson, 2018, p. 8, emphasis added). Yet form is not identical to the *individual* substance, which depends upon matter.[32]

Koons has constructed a transformative version of hylomorphism which offers an analytic way to cash out these claims in terms of contemporary *trope theory* (Koons, 2022).[33] According to trope theorists, the world is made up of many particulars (tropes), such as the particular shape, the particular colour, or the particular texture of a concrete individual entity. For two entities to share the same property, such as the property of whiteness, for example, is for them both to exemplify a trope of whiteness. Although these tropes are numerically distinct, they are said to *exactly resemble* each other. Thus similarity and difference between two concrete particulars is to be explained in terms of resemblance (or lack of resemblance) between the respective tropes of which they are comprised.

Koons distinguishes between modular tropes, which are self-exemplifying, and modifying tropes, which lack this peculiarity. A modular trope of F may be said to have F itself, where F might be a trope of whiteness, whereas a modifying trope may only be said to *confer* the property of whiteness. Since forms are modifying tropes, in Koons's view, the accidental form of whiteness is not itself white. Likewise, since substantial forms are modifying tropes, the substantial form which is Socrates' soul, considered apart from Socrates' matter, is not itself an individual human being (a substance).

Trope resemblance, according to Koons, is properly analysed in terms of *grounded numerical distinctness*. Two substantial forms may be said to belong to the same *species* just in case their numerical distinctness is not metaphysically fundamental but is derived from the numerical distinctness of some class of 'prime-material' entities (Koons, 2022, p. 11).[34] Socrates' and Plato's substantial forms, for example, are not distinct *of themselves*, according to Koons's

---

[32] Many think that a substance depends upon matter for its individuation, although some would argue that individual substantial forms individuate substances.

[33] For an introduction to the conception of properties as tropes, see Heil (2012, chp. 2).

[34] Jeffrey Brower has arrived independently at a view of the nature and function of prime matter that is similar to the view which has recently been advanced by Koons (Brower, 2017).

metaphysical account, but are only distinct in virtue of the prior numerical distinctness of the two portions of prime matter that they are said to in-form.

Likewise, two substantial forms which belong to the same *genus* but different species must be individuated by their respective differentiae. If a substantial form *F* belongs to some genus *G*, then that form has to 'express' itself through one of a class of proper accidents *P* (or propria, to use scholastic parlance),[35] where each member of this class is said to be 'contrary' to the others, and where it is impossible for the substantial form to change this mode of expression. On this view, it is the proper accidents, rather than the substantial forms, which are fundamentally distinct from one another, and the fact that two forms belong to different species is grounded in the numerical distinctness of the differentiae.[36]

Prime matter, then, whilst having no intrinsic nature of its own, has a fundamental role to play in *individuating* substances of the same species, whilst substantial form has a fundamental role to play in conferring a nature. In this way, we can see how prime matter and substantial form may be said to complete one another, whilst neither can count as individual substances in their own right. Considered separately, 'prime matter is fundamentally particular but derivatively natured while form is fundamentally natured but derivatively particular' (Koons, 2022, p. 29). Taken together, prime matter and substantial form achieve something which is 'derivatively natured and derivatively particular' when they complete one another by composing a hylomorphic substance (Koons, 2022).

In what sense, then, are hylomorphic substances *fundamental* entities, if they *derive* both their natures and their particularity from their matter and form? They are fundamental, one might say, in the sense that there is no change in the physical world in which scientists conduct their experiments that does not involve change in a physical substance. According to Schaffer's 'tiling constraint', every physical part of nature should be wholly contained in the sum of its substances, and no two substances should overlap (Schaffer, 2010). Unlike Schaffer, however, Koons offers a hylomorphic analysis of *physical* substances in terms of their *metaphysical* constituents of matter and form.

Contrary to Jaworski, Koons rejects the identification of matter with a physical stuff whose nature is disclosed by our best physics, but which may or may not be part of a hylomorphic composite. 'If there are enduring entities with their own natures, independent of the action of substantial forms, then any change is fundamentally merely an alteration of those same enduring entities'

---

[35] The concept of propria is further discussed in Section 4.

[36] Only in the case of substantial forms which belong to different genera of the highest level may their numerical distinctness be taken as fundamental (that is, as ungrounded).

(Koons, 2022, p. 24–5). Instead of identifying prime matter as physical stuff, he embraces a metaphysical conception of matter in terms of a 'gunky continuum' which has infinitely many parts but lacks an enduring physical nature (Koons, 2022, p. 24). These prime-material entities individuate every part of a physical substance and provide a substrate for substantial change,[37] but they are not identical to the particles (or fields) of contemporary particle physics.[38]

Contrary to Marmodoro, Koons insists that a substantial form can be the *cause* of a substance being what it is without violating the *unity* of the substance by being (in a univocal sense) 'part' of what it is supposed to unify. We might get a handle on his position by considering an analogy. Suppose I imagine a triangle whose sides are in the ratio of the integers 3:4:5 (that is, a 3-4-5 Pythagorean triple). The imagined triangle is a compound containing four entities: my act of imagination, and the three lines of the triangle, which are each of distinct lengths. On the one hand, there is clearly a difference between the way in which my act of imagination is part of the imagined triangle, and the way in which each of the distinct objects imagined (the lines) are parts. On the other hand, all four of these elements are distinct and disjoint constituents of a single whole. The two sorts of elements composing this whole – namely, my act of imagination, and the three lines – are not of the same ontological standing, since my act of imagination explains why the lines of the triangle exist in the first place. Analogously, a substantial form can be *united* with a collection of prime-material constituents by being the *formal cause* of the whole.

Koons's constituent-based hylomorphism thus admits substances which have an internal ontological complexity that is prohibited by Marmodoro's concept-based hylomorphism (see Table 3). For Koons, a substance has a finite number of *integral* parts, which are necessarily *actual* rather than potential parts. An actual part is an integral part if its individual identity is tied to the identity of the substance that contains it in such a way that this part can neither exist as a substance in its own right nor as a part of a different substance. Yet an integral part, such as a man's hand, may be said to have a nature which grounds certain active and passive causal powers. In other words, a substance can have actual parts which objectively exist and possess their own peculiar causal powers.

---

[37] Koons speculates that prime-material lack any modal or temporal properties of their own, yet entities composed of prime-material may persist in a derived way in virtue of their substantial forms. He suggests we model this form of persistence using the *genidentity relation* (Reichenbach, 1956). It seems an alternative version could be given, however, in which it persists fundamentally.

[38] In Section 3, I shall discuss how his theory may connect with contemporary physics.

Table 3 A classification of the different types of parts of a biological substance in Koons's transformative, constituent-based account of hylomorphism

Classifying parts of a biological substance		
	Integral	**Non-Integral**
Actual	Cells, organs, tissues, atoms, molecules – when activated	Prime matter
Potential	Particles, atoms, molecules – when not activated	Inorganic substances in organisms

A substance can also have actual parts which are *non-integral* parts. The bits of prime matter that individuate a physical substance, unlike its integral parts, can belong to different substances at different times (and in different possible worlds). Unlike integral parts, however, they have no nature or causal powers of their own. So the actual parts of a substance, whether they are integral or non-integral parts of the substance, do not count as substances in their own right, and hence the metaphysical unity of the substance as a whole is preserved.

Substances also admit an infinite number of *potential* parts. There are potential parts which are *integral* parts of a substance, having no actual existence within the substance unless they are 'activated' within the whole through some intervention (for example, during a scientific experiment), but which do not count as substances in their own right. There are also *potential* parts that are *non-integral* parts of a substance: that is, parts which have no actual existence within the substance as long as it remains whole, but which do not depend for their identities upon the substance as a whole, such as the various substances into which a biological organism may degenerate when it dies. In spite of all of this internal complexity, however, the unity of a substance is preserved, in the non-univocal sense in which Koons conceives of being and unity.

Koons's transformative hylomorphism thus preserves a unifying role for substantial form that is precluded by Jaworski's structural hylomorphism. For Koons, the proper parts of a substance have no definitionally independent, determinate causal powers. The matter of a substance does not consist of entities described by our best physics, which supposedly retain the same physical powers within a substance that they possess in the wild. Rather, the powers of the parts of the substance depend for their definition upon the substance as a whole, which owes its nature to its substantial form. The unity of the composite thus derives from the unity of the substantial form, which grounds all its essential causal powers.

There is no question that Koons's theory of hylomorphism is more extravagant than Jaworski's or Marmodoro's. It also breaks with a post-Quinean orthodoxy of conceiving the world in terms of fundamental physical constituents, by adopting a metaphysical conception of matter and form. As I noted, many philosophers think we should not posit a more metaphysical conception of matter because they believe modern physics has revealed – or will someday uncover – the basic stuff of which everything is made. This is one reason why some hylomorphists prefer structural versions of hylomorphism rather than transformative versions. Other philosophers, however, have questioned whether physics uncovers any kind of stuff which could serve as a material substrate.[39] In the following section, we will consider the challenge that powerist, constituent-based hylomorphic theories face from Jaegwon Kim's causal exclusion dilemma, and why a *transformative* version of hylomorphism may be needed to explain how complex substances, like biological substances, can make a causal difference in the physical world.

3 What Physics Means for Hylomorphism

Of the three powerist hylomorphic theories that I discussed in some detail in the previous section, only the two constituent-based hylomorphic accounts purported to treat living organisms as substances which exist and sustain themselves independently of our conceptual activities. In these accounts, a substantial form generates a composite entity (a substance) from a material substrate yet is immanent to the substance that it generates. In this section, I will discuss a second challenge that these two hylomorphic accounts face in seeking to carve an ontology of biological substances which have irreducible powers, namely: the challenge of explaining how these substances can make a *causal difference* in the physical world without recourse to dualism or physicalism.

Are Emergent Powers Excluded?   We are seeking hylomorphic accounts which can ground a real distinction between living organisms and heaps of matter. According to Koons's and Jaworski's constituent-based hylomorphisms, biological substances must include among their basic constituents a 'form' (or 'structure') which confers upon the parts of the substance the distinctive properties of a living organism. These properties of the whole are considered to be novel with respect to (or unpredictable on the basis of) our knowledge of the properties of any of its physical parts taken in isolation. Moreover, they are supposed to introduce new causal powers which are not reducible to the powers of its physical parts.

---

[39] For example, see Simpson (2020), Simpson (2021b), and Section 3.

To avoid confusing hylomorphism with some kind of vitalistic dualism, however, we should not think of the substantial form that unifies a composite, such as a living organism, as operating like a Cartesian soul by pushing its parts around. A Cartesian soul is a separate substance from the material body that it manipulates. Rather, we should think of the causal powers of a composite substance as in some sense *emerging* from – or being partly grounded in – its material parts. Living organisms are 'processual-emergents', to use Walsh's term, which display a 'reciprocity between system and component' (Walsh & Wiebe, 2020, p. 111). Yet this requirement seems to lay constituent-based hylomorphism open to Jaegwon Kim's causal exclusion problem (Kim, 1999).

The original context of Kim's objection is the problem of mental causation. Briefly, Kim assumes that, in order to be realists about mental properties, we must find causal work for them to do. The problem arises in trying to reconcile the causal powers attributed to mental properties with the supposed 'causal closure of the physical', which is the requirement that any physical event that has a cause at time *t* must have a *physical* cause at *t* (a claim which dualists deny). The problem I wish to discuss is more general than the problem of mental causation. As Kim notes, it attaches to the 'diachronic causal influence of [higher-level] emergent phenomena on lower-level phenomena' (Kim, 1999, p. 32).

As Kim notes, the idea that there are emergent properties in nature can be traced back to John Stuart Mill's distinction between the 'homopathic' laws he believed govern mechanical phenomena, which are based on vector or algebraic addition, and the 'heteropathic' laws he believed govern chemical phenomena, which cannot be deduced from homopathic laws. Today, the relevant distinction is drawn between *weak emergence*, which 'requires that higher-level properties have a proper subset of the token powers of their dependence base features' (a view associated with non-reductive physicalism), and *strong emergence*, which 'requires that higher-level features have more token powers than their dependence base features' (a view which recalls British emergentism) (Wilson, 2015). Kim thinks that reduction – broadly conceived – fails only if higher-level properties introduce new causal powers, but he doubts whether they do so.

Let's consider the generalised version of Kim's causal exclusion problem for some higher-level property E_1 of an emergent whole.[40] If E_1 is causally powerful, it can cause some other higher-level property E_2 to obtain. This is an instance of *same-level causation*. Since E_1 and E_2 are both emergent properties, we must suppose that E_1 emerges from some basal condition B_1, and that E_2

---

[40] See also the discussion of this problem in Tabaczek (2019) and Walsh and Wiebe (2020).

emerges from some basal physical state B_2.[41] Moreover, since E_2 emerges from B_2, we must suppose that E_2 will obtain whenever B_2 obtains, and that E_2 will obtain whether or not the higher-level property E_1 obtains. There is no way that E_1 can cause E_2 without bringing about B_2, Kim argues, since the only way in which E_2 can obtain is by emerging from the basal physical state B_2. It seems, then, that the only way in which E_1 can cause E_2 is by E_1 causing the basal physical state B_2 to obtain. In other words, same-level causation of one higher-level property by another entails *top-down causation*.

The question is why cannot B_1 displace E_1 as the *cause* of B_2? Recall that E_1's causation of the higher-level property E_2 presupposes E_1's top-down causation of the basal property B_2, and that E_1 is supposed to emerge from the basal physical state B_1. Kim conceives causation as nomological sufficiency. Since B_1 as E_1's emergence base is assumed to be nomologically sufficient for E_1 (an assumption I will challenge presently, in the light of quantum mechanics), and since E_1 as B_2's cause is likewise assumed to be nomologically sufficient for B_2, it follows that B_1 is nomologically sufficient for B_2. So we may conceive B_1 as its cause. The same conclusion follows if causation is construed in terms of counterfactuals (that is, as a condition without which the consequent would not have occurred). Doesn't that make E_1 causally redundant?

Kim believes it would be a mistake to think of E_1 as being an intermediate link in a causal chain leading from B_1 to B_2, and therefore as an ontologically distinct member of that causal chain. To avoid dualism, E_1 is supposed to depend for its physical being upon B_1, and so E_1 cannot be assigned the same ontological status as the basal conditions B_1 and B_2, as if it were a separate link in the chain. It seems that if the higher-level property E_1 is to be retained as a *cause* of B_2, we are faced with the consequence that top-down causation from E_1 to B_2 involves *causal overdetermination*, since B_1 is (also) the cause of B_2.

What should we conclude about the causal powers of higher-level properties? Unless we are willing to accept causal overdetermination, Kim argues, we should reject the possibility of top-down causation. Yet if we reject the possibility of top-down causation, we must reject the *emergence* of higher-level properties which have irreducible causal powers of their own. Kim thinks the implausibility of causal overdetermination outweighs the plausibility of top-down causation. The causal efficacy of higher-level properties, if they exist, is thus excluded.

Kim's argument is not watertight. Its original formulation seems to depend upon a number of assumptions about causation and emergence one might call into question. For instance, in addition to assuming that B_1 is nomologically

---

[41] Or from one of a set of basal conditions $B_{1,2}$ if $E_{1,2}$ is multiply realisable.

sufficient for E_1, and that higher-level properties supervene upon lower-level properties, Kim also seems to assume that if E_2 emerges from B_2, then something can cause E_2 only by *causing B_2*. None of these assumptions seems beyond question, and indeed I will be questioning some of them in what follows. Nonetheless, determining exactly where Kim's argument goes astray – if it does go astray – and providing a positive consensual account of higher-level powers has not proven an easy task for contemporary emergentists.

Kim's causal exclusion problem also seems to present constituent-based hylomorphists with a troubling dilemma: either the higher-level properties of a whole are epiphenomenal, in which case a powerist ought to drop them from their ontology, or, the higher-level properties are reducible, in which case they are not 'higher-level' in any *ontological* sense, since they represent no addition to being over and above the lower-level properties of a substance's parts.[42] Either way, how is a biological substance such as a living organism supposed to make a causal difference to the physical world *qua* biological substance? It seems that all of the causal work is being done by its physical parts, in which case, we should drop the composite whole from our fundamental ontology.

Does Causal Pluralism Trump Causal Closure?   Perhaps surprisingly, Jaworski rejects top-down causation, in spite of his ontological commitment to biological substances with irreducible causal powers. In fact, he thinks his version of structural hylomorphism has an advantage because it does not require it. When Jaworski claims that structure 'operates as an irreducible ontological principle' (Jaworski, 2016, p. 17), he does not mean to suggest that structures produce some new kind of force which causes matter to move in ways that it otherwise would not. In his view, hylomorphism is compatible with 'all forces operating at a fundamental physical level' (Jaworski, 2011, p. 291); that is, below the composite level at which things get structured.

Although Jaworski thinks that a 'super-physicist' could in principle provide us with a true description of the world that tells us where all of the matter ends up, however, he believes this description would be missing some important details – such as the difference between the living and non-living (Jaworski, 2016, p. 10). What she would be missing are the *structures* that confer upon these things certain additional properties, over and above the properties of their physical constituents. Structural hylomorphists may embrace the supervenience of higher levels upon lower levels, but they should reject 'lower-level determination' (Jaworski, 2016, p. 287) since higher-level properties perform different explanatory roles.

---

[42] I take it that Marmodoro's concept-based hylomorphism, discussed in the previous section, does not face this particular objection, since she denies that substances have actual parts.

Jaworski thinks this simple appeal to *explanatory pluralism* is sufficient to overcome Kim's causal exclusion objection (Jaworski, 2016, pp. 280–5), once we have understood the explanatory role that is played by his conception of structure. The higher-level powers of a composite, which it possesses in virtue of its structure, are supposed to figure in different kinds of explanations than the lower-level powers of its physical parts, which determine where its matter ends up according to lower-level laws. For example, on one level of explanation, it is true that the kettle in my kitchen boiled because a nerve impulse was sent out from a cell body in my brain triggering a physiological mechanism in which my right forefinger flipped the switch on the kettle. On another level, it is equally true that the kettle boiled because I was thirsty and chose to make tea. The first explanation concerns how the motion of my body was performed; the second concerns my rational motivations for performing an action. The second explanation, one might urge, is concerned with a different kind of question.

Yet here is a point of tension in Jaworski's theory of hylomorphism: why should 'structured' composites, like organisms, be attributed being alongside simple entities, like electrons, if they lack top-down causal powers to make a difference to the motion of their own parts? According to the Eleatic Principle – which Jaworski endorses – whatever has *being* is supposed to be *powerful*. Yet hylomorphic composites, as Jaworski conceives them, lack any 'force-generating properties' to change how the matter flows through them (Jaworski, 2011, p. 290), on pain of introducing new forces within nature unknown to our best physics, such as vital forces in biology, and hence of 'violating. . . the causal closure of the physical domain' – something he insists that structural hylomorphists 'cannot reject' (Jaworski, 2011, p. 345). So why do composites get to be part of the ontology?

The key move which Jaworski makes in order to secure the powerfulness of higher-level properties, whilst shunning vitalistic forms of dualism, is to identify *explanatory* irreducibility with *causal* irreducibility, and hence explanatory pluralism with causal pluralism. There are different ways in which something can be a cause besides being a *physical* cause. The powerfulness of higher-level properties, and hence the ontological significance of structure, is thus supposed to rest upon the *autonomy* of such explanations (Robinson, 2014).

It is not clear, however, that this move is well-motivated. A physicalist may admit that the concept of structure plays an essential role within the explanatory practices of the special sciences, and be willing to grant that something which is essential to explanation should be conceived realistically. It does not follow, however, that the only way to conceive an entity or property *realistically* is to make it part of one's *fundamental* ontology on a level with physical matter, especially if that entity or property contributes nothing to the motion of physical matter over and above the fundamental forces of physics. After all, one can formulate useful 'higher-level' rules about the behaviour of cellular patterns in Conway's 'Game of Life', which refer to structural features of those entities that are grounded in the spatiotemporal distribution of their parts, even though the simple 'lower-level' rules which govern the evolution of the cells in the computer program make no reference to such properties and are deterministic.

It is also unclear how this appeal to explanatory pluralism is supposed to solve the causal exclusion problem. Since the forces that govern where matter ends up are (supposedly) operating at a microphysical level, and since structure cannot make a causal difference to *where* matter flows within a composite of microphysical stuff without introducing non-physical forces, it seems an *embodied action* which involves the *motion of matter* will have to be explained as the manifestations of two autonomous and complete sets of powers. Consider again my action of making a cup of tea. First, we would have to say, there are the powers of the lower-level (physical) properties, which determine the *motion* described by the laws of physics; second, the powers of the higher-level (mental) properties, which determine the rational character of my *action*. Yet it is difficult to make sense of how two sets of *complete* and *autonomous* powers are supposed to determine the embodied action of a *single* substance.

On the one hand, a dualist who accepts the hypothesis of psychophysical parallelism can explain how the two sets of powers could be complete and autonomous, but at the cost of denying that they determine the action of a *single* entity. A parallelist may regard the two sets of powers to be *complete*, in the sense that each set is sufficient of itself to determine the behaviour of a different entity: one completely determines the physical behaviour of my material body, and the other completely determines the rational behaviour of my immaterial mind. And a parallelist may consider the two sets of powers to be *autonomous* because God has ordained a pre-established harmony between them, such that my mental and physical properties are correlated even though my mind lacks any force-generating properties to 'interfere' with the motion of my body's matter.

On the other hand, a physicalist who rejects microphysical reduction can explain how the two sets of powers could be exercised by a *single* entity in performing a single action, but at the cost of denying that the higher-level powers are *complete*. A physicalist may regard the lower powers to be complete and autonomous, because the lower-level powers of my physical parts determine the motion of my matter according to physical laws which are causally closed. And a non-reductive physicalist who admits weak emergence can explain how there are higher-level properties that belong to the same entity, but only by denying that they are ultimately determinative of that entity's behaviour: the higher-level powers are merely a *subset* of the lower-level powers of their emergence base. Although we may find it necessary to conceptualise the behaviour of complex entities in terms of higher-level properties, such explanations involve a *subtraction* from being, rather than an addition to being.

To take either of these paths, however, would be to reject Jaworski's account of hylomorphism, since in both cases structure would be deprived of its basic role in objectively carving the world into substances. But how does Jaworski expect us to tread a straight path between them? Unlike some physicalists, he cannot appeal to the fact that physical properties are the *most fundamental* in order to explain why the lower-level (physical) powers determine the motion of my matter in an autonomous way that excludes top-down causation – not without threatening the *fundamentality* of substance. Unlike some dualists, he cannot appeal to a pre-established harmony to account for how the higher-level (mental) powers could determine the rational character of my action without imposing any force upon the motion of my matter – not without dissolving the *unity* of the substance that is supposed to perform the embodied action.

What is needed, I suggest – but what Jaworski's theory of hylomorphism precludes – is an account of how higher- and lower-level powers *complete one another* in determining the motion and action of a single substance. It is precluded because he treats every substance as consisting of the same physical stuff, having the same lower-level, force-generating powers to determine the motion of matter within a substance that they possess in the wild.

Is Causal Closure Scientifically Motivated?   Kim's causal exclusion argument is a manifestation of a more entrenched orthodoxy of contemporary philosophy concerning the relation between physics and metaphysics, which rules against the existence of fundamental, macroscopic entities with higher-level causal powers (Simpson, 2022; Simpson & Horsley, 2022). To begin with, it is widely supposed among analytic metaphysicians that our 'best physics' specifies a set of *universal* laws for the temporal development of matter, and that to offer an interpretation of a physical theory is to identify the set of worlds that are possible according to that theory. On this view, a possible world is a complete and internally consistent possible state of affairs, and a physical theory contributes to our knowledge of nature by declaring some of these states permissible whilst excluding others. The universal laws which are specified by this theory determine the set of possible worlds.

According to standard post-Quinean metaphysics, the task of interpreting a physical theory involves identifying some set of physical constituents to which this theory refers, and elucidating their possible arrangements according to this theory's laws. The basic constituents may be microscopic entities or modifications of a single substance. Either way, the total set of their physically possible arrangements determines the 'state space' within which the physical state of the cosmos evolves. Having identified these basic physical constituents, propositions about the physical world may be evaluated as true or false just in case they can be understood as referring to their physically possible arrangements. Ruetsche describes this nomological notion of physical possibility as a *unimodal* conception of possibility: on this view, 'everything that is physically possible must be possible in the same way' (Ruetsche, 2011, p. 3).

This unimodal conception of possibility is often united with some form of ontological reductionism. It is presupposed by microphysicalists, for example, who favour the ontological priority of the microscopic. It is presupposed by priority monists, who believe microscopic reality is grounded in the cosmos as a whole (Schaffer, 2010). Microphysicalists and priority monists are divided concerning the number of fundamental entities, but united in excluding from the fundamental ontology any entities that exist between the microscopic or the cosmic scale. In their hierarchical and reductionist picture of the physical world, higher levels are supposed to be related to lower levels in such a way that the physical content of a higher-level theory can be derived from the physical content of a lower-level theory (Leggett, 1992).

This unimodal conception of physical possibility is also compatible with the theory of weak emergence, which rejects strong forms of ontological reduction. Weak emergentists regard higher-level causal powers as a subset of the lower-level causal powers of their emergence base (Bedau, 1997), whilst attributing failures in reduction to our epistemic limitations. Since weak emergentists affirm the supervenience of higher-level laws and properties upon lower-level laws and properties, they must also affirm that the set of physical possibilities is 'closed' under the lower-level laws. To think otherwise, it is commonly supposed, is to introduce 'spooky' forces within nature of which physics knows nothing.

Although this assumption may be deeply ingrained within the thinking of many analytic philosophers like Kim and Jaworski, however, and may make sense of a world made of microscopic corpuscles governed by mechanical forces, it has the appearance of being an *imposition* upon the theory of quantum mechanics, which is our best theory of the behaviour of physical matter. The notorious 'measurement problem' of quantum mechanics, which continues to exercise philosophers and physicists who study the foundations of physics, remains an open problem in the interpretation of quantum mechanics precisely because of the role that *macroscopic* measurements seem to play in modifying the *microscopic* behaviour of physical systems (Schlosshauer, 2005).

The fundamental mathematical object within standard quantum theory is the wave function – or, more properly, the quantum state of the system $|\psi\rangle$ – which encodes the probability of an arbitrarily complicated physical system having a particular configuration. Prior to any measurement of a physical system, the wave function, according to standard quantum mechanics, evolves according to the time-dependent Schrödinger equation:

$$\hat{H}|\psi\rangle = i\hbar\frac{\partial|\psi\rangle}{\partial t}, \tag{3.1}$$

where $\hat{H}$ is the Hamiltonian of the system, which represents its energy. Equation (3.1) admits a formal solution in terms of a unitary operator $\hat{U}$:

$$|\psi(t)\rangle = \hat{U}(t)|\psi(0)\rangle. \tag{3.2}$$

This equation tells us that the wave function at some arbitrary time t can be obtained from the wave function at time $t = 0$ through the action of the operator $\hat{U}$. By calling it a 'unitary' operator, I mean that probabilities computed from the wave function $|\psi\rangle$ will always sum to unity, because the operator $\hat{U}$ merely re-distributes the probabilities between different possibilities as time elapses. This theory tells us how to start from a given state of a system and evolve the probability amplitudes for all the possible configurations of the system in time.[43]

But suppose we perform what is called a 'non-demolition' measurement on the system, which does not destroy the quantum system being measured. For example, suppose we try to measure the number of photons in an electromagnetic wave (Dong et al., 2008). After this measurement, we know something more about the physical state of this system than the information contained in the wave function (3.2): the measurement outcome of the experiment may, with certainty, have ruled out some of the states to which $|\psi\rangle$ assigns a non-zero probability. To obtain the correct results for future experiments we have to *update* the wave function with the empirical knowledge we have gained.

The difficulty that quantum theory presents to Kim's conception of the causal closure of the physical domain, in which the lower-level, microscopic causal powers of a physical system are supposed to determine how this physical system evolves, is that this updating of the wave function is not automatically performed by the time evolution operator $\hat{U}$ that embodies Schrödinger's law. For instance, suppose at time t we find an electromagnetic field has n photons

---

[43] In fact, during the course of its evolution, a wave function becomes superpositions of possible configurations which are said to 'interfere' with one another, such that statistical predictions of quantum mechanics cannot be understood in terms of the statistics of a proper mixture.

in it, $|\psi\rangle = |n\rangle$. To match up the quantum mechanical description of the system, going forward, with the results of our experiment, the wave function of the system is said to have undergone the following modification, making it discontinuous with the wave function previously used to describe the system just prior to t:

$$
\begin{aligned}
|\psi(t - \delta t)\rangle &= \hat{U}(t - \delta t)|\psi(0)\rangle, \\
|\psi(t + \delta t)\rangle &= |n\rangle.
\end{aligned}
\tag{3.3}
$$

This discontinuous change is known as the 'collapse of the wave function', and it is necessary to accept this change in order to account for the different measurement outcomes of any non-demolition experiment. Unfortunately, there is no agreed understanding of how the process of wave function collapse is supposed to take place (Omnès, 1994).[44]

The measurement problem, to put it another way, is the problem of how quantum systems evolve from states that are spread out (that is, states which are *superpositions* with respect to some variable that scientists are interested in measuring) to states which are localised (that is, states which are *determinate* with respect to that variable). It calls for an interpretation of quantum mechanics in order to make sense of a scientist's experience of a world in which macroscopic measuring devices are seen to register determinate measurement outcomes.

According to the physicist John Bell, any realist approach to quantum mechanics that seeks to reconcile the existence of determinate measurement outcomes with quantum mechanics confronts a dilemma: either the dynamics of standard quantum mechanics is wrong, and the wave function evolves in a way that permits it to collapse into a state that involves determinate values for the variable being measured; or standard quantum mechanics is incomplete in its description of physical reality, and there are 'hidden variables' that encode the determinate outcomes of quantum experiments (Bell, 1987).

The philosopher of science, Tim Maudlin, has argued that, of the many and varied proposals that have been offered so far, there seem to be two sensible options for philosophers to consider: either we should adopt something like the GRW theory of the collapse of the wave function or something like the theory of Bohmian mechanics (Maudlin, 1995). Both solutions presuppose a nomological conception of possibility in which the temporal development of the physical world is closed under universal laws, and both solutions have to

---

[44] Even if the phenomenon of decoherence is taken into account (as suggested in e.g. (Omnès, 1994)), the time evolution operator must still be supplemented with a discontinuous change of state.

modify standard quantum mechanics in somewhat ad hoc ways in order to produce theories which can specify *universal* laws for quantum systems that do not depend upon the existence of a macroscopic 'observer'.

First, the GRW model suggested by the physicists Giancarlo Ghirardi, Alberto Rimini, and Tullio Weber in 1986 supplements standard quantum mechanics with a stochastic mechanism which produces random 'hits' on the wave function that occur universally for microscopic particles and which result in an objective collapse of the wave function (Ghirardi, Rimini, & Weber, 1986). These spontaneous collapses happen so rarely, however, that we can never hope to detect them. Yet the effects of this rather contrived modification of the Schrödinger dynamics of the wave function become significant when a large number of entangled particles are involved, such as the particles that compose a macroscopic instrument of measurement. That is why a macroscopic system, according to the GRW solution to the measurement problem, is a well-localised entity – at least, for all practical purposes. And that is why, according to the Bohmian solution, a macroscopic measuring device can register determinate outcomes in an experiment.

Second, the pilot wave theory conceived by the physicists Louis de Broglie and David Bohm (which has been championed by Detlef Dürr, Sheldon Goldstein, and Nino Zanghi under the name of 'Bohmian mechanics' since the 1990s) posits a global configuration of particles whose definite positions are governed by a supplementary guiding equation (de Broglie, 1928; Bohm, 1951, 1952). This guiding equation depends in a non-linear way upon a 'universal wave function' that evolves according to the standard Schrödinger equation, and which is not subject to any ad hoc mechanisms for spontaneous collapse. However, the Bohmian particles have to be initially distributed in just the right way, in order to achieve empirical equivalence with standard quantum mechanics, and this fine-tuning condition has also been criticised for being contrived. Macroscopic objects, like measuring devices, are made of these Bohmian particles, which always have definite positions, however 'spread out' the wave function guiding their evolution may happen to be. And that is why, according to the Bohmian solution, a macroscopic system such as a measuring device is well-localised and can register determinate outcomes.

An alternative solution to the troublesome measurement problem of quantum mechanics is available, however, which offers a different model of the quantum dynamics that is derived from the theory of open quantum systems. This model drops the assumption that the temporal development of every microscopic system in nature is causally closed under exactly the same microscopic dynamics. According to 'CWC theory' (contextual wave function collapse theory), which was recently proposed by the physicist Barbara Drossel and the cosmologist

George Ellis, quantum systems are causally open to their 'classical' environments. It is the interaction of a quantum system with the intrinsic heat bath of a finite-temperature, macroscopic system within its environment that causes the collapse of its wave function (Drossel & Ellis, 2018).

Like GRW theory, CWC theory seizes the first horn of Bell's dilemma, allowing the wave function of a microscopic system to collapse. Unlike GRW theory, however, the stochastic corrections that collapse the wave function depend upon the *macroscopic context* of the system. In short, the CWC model incorporates a feedback loop – from a particle, via the intrinsic heat bath of the measuring device, back to the particle – which introduces non-linear terms in the Schrödinger equation governing the evolution of the system that are specific to the system's context. CWC theory thus avoids introducing an ad hoc collapse mechanism into quantum mechanics in order to explain the localisation of the wave function, since these extra terms can be accounted for in terms of thermodynamics and solid-state physics (Drossel & Ellis, 2018, pp. 13–19).

Whilst CWC theory is empirically equivalent to other interpretations of quantum mechanics, it implies that the world is *not* a single closed system which evolves according to universal laws. Rather, the world contains 'open' quantum systems whose temporal development is *context-dependent*. These quantum systems are embedded in 'classical' environments, which are characterised by higher-level properties that are not governed by quantum laws and make a difference to the dynamics of quantum systems. They derive these causal powers from the role they play in defining the Hilbert spaces and time scales in which the unitary time evolution of an open quantum system takes place.[45]

Ellis believes that the interface between the microscopic (quantum) and mesoscopic (thermal) levels offers a pattern for how things work in nature at multiple levels, including the interface between the physical and the chemical and the interface between the chemical and the biological.[46] If something like Ellis's conception of how higher-level structure shapes outcomes at lower-levels is in fact the case, where higher-level structures always impose constraints upon lower-level dynamics, then it is a mistake to think of the forces that determine where matter ends up as operating solely at a fundamental physical level according to universal laws, and a fumble to suppose that everything is made out of a determinate physical stuff which has the same force-generating

---

[45] For further philosophical discussion of this theory in relation to hylomorphism, see Simpson (2020) and Simpson (2021b).

[46] For further discussion of how higher-level structure constrains lower-level physics, see Ellis (2021) and Simpson and Horsley (2022).

powers independently of its physical context. Rather, higher-level powers are implicated in *all* motion and lower-level powers are *never* sufficient to determine where matter ends up. If something like this conception of how physics relates to the 'special' sciences is true, then Kim's causal exclusion problem – and Jaworski's theory of hylomorphism – rests on a conception of matter that is false.

How Can Hylomorphism Make Sense of Emergence? After quantum mechanics, I suggest, philosophers need no longer treat the causal closure of the microphysical domain as sacrosanct. Indeed, every attempt to reconcile this metaphysical dogma with the theory of quantum mechanics demands considerable ingenuity and comes with theoretical costs. As we have seen, there is an alternative contextual interpretation of quantum mechanics which admits top-down causation. Whilst CWC theory shuns the causal closure of the microscopic, it raises metaphysical questions concerning how the microscopic world of quantum systems and the macroscopic world of their measuring devices are supposed to be related: for instance, how are properties like temperature and chemical entropy, which characterise an open quantum system's environment, supposed to 'emerge' from a microscopic base?

On the one hand, suppose the causal powers of every macroscopic system could ultimately be explained in terms of the causal powers of its microscopic base. In that case, it would seem that the environment of a microscopic quantum system does not contain any macroscopic entities which have novel powers that make a difference to its temporal development. Yet CWC theory does not appear to be compatible with microphysical reductionism, since it provides the macroscopic, thermal properties of a measuring device with a fundamental role to play in collapsing the wave function of a microscopic quantum system, thus endowing higher-level, macroscopic properties with top-down causal powers.

On the other hand, suppose that the existence and properties of a macroscopic system, from one moment to the next, were not in any way dependent upon the activity of any microscopic parts, whilst such a system had novel and irreducible powers to act upon microscopic entities and cause them to change their collective behaviour. In that case, there would be good reason to count such a macroscopic system as a distinct entity that *interacts* with other microscopic entities rather than being *composed* of them (Gillett, 2016, p. 247). Yet CWC theory does not lend itself to a fundamental dualism of microscopic and macroscopic physical entities either, since it only characterises the behaviour of microscopic entities within particular macroscopic contexts.

It might be tempting to dismiss CWC theory as lacking any ontology *tout court*. However, there is a third possibility: the priority of the macrophysical.

On this view, the macrophysical entity is the fundamental physical entity, and the powers of its microscopic parts are grounded in the macroscopic entity as a whole. Koons's theory of 'staunch hylomorphism' may offer a way of cashing out the relations between the macroscopic whole and its microscopic parts (Koons, 2014), though it has to be modified somewhat in the light of his more recent work (Koons, 2022).[47] In this account, the persistence of a whole is grounded in an ongoing cooperation between its integral parts,[48] whilst the active and passive powers of the integral parts are grounded in corresponding primary powers of the whole. This version of hylomorphism may be compatible with CWC theory (as I have argued elsewhere), providing a way of understanding how a macroscopic substance with top-down causal powers might be said to 'emerge' from the activity of a material substrate (Simpson, 2021b).[49]

In the first place, microphysicalism is averted because the microscopic powers of the substance must be *grounded* in the substance as a whole at every moment. The only primary powers which matter may be said to possess, independently of any substance, are powers to be determined in different ways within different substances. Any secondary powers which a parcel of matter may possess, in virtue of being an actual, integral part of a substance, are determined by the substantial form of the substance. Adapting an earlier definition given by Koons, let us say that a physical entity x is an *instrument* of a substance y at some instant of time t just in case: for every significant active or passive power P of x, there is some power P' of y such that P is grounded in P', and the exercise of P at t would contribute to some natural end of y (Koons, 2014, p. 172).[50]

Koons's hylomorphism thus introduces a synchronic, top-down dependency relation between a whole and its integral parts, in which the whole is said to 'instrumentalise' its parts. This seems to be the correct direction for this dependency: if the powers of the whole were synchronically grounded in the powers of its proper parts, then the whole could not be said to act upon its parts

---

[47] Koons's recent work on hylomorphism has, in my judgement, departed in certain ways from his earlier work on 'staunch' hylomorphism. In his earlier work (Koons, 2014), form was conceived as a process and the matter of a substance was to some degree physicalised, whereas in his later work (Koons, 2022), form is conceived as a trope and matter is entirely metaphysical. Henceforward, I shall drop the label 'staunch', classifying his theory in terms of my own taxonomy (Table 1). I shall also take the top-down and bottom-up dependency relations described in the earlier theory to be relations that obtain between the *integral* parts of the substance and the substantial whole.

[48] See Table 3 for a classification of different types of parts.

[49] In the metaphysical interpretation of CWC theory I put forward in Simpson (2021b), the inorganic world consists of 'thermal substances', as Koons has suggested elsewhere (Koons, 2019).

[50] In Koons's original definition in Koons (2014), the power P is only *partly* grounded in P'.

without falling into a vicious causal circularity, leading us back into the arms of the microphysicalist. For Koons, the proper parts of a substance can have no independent and determinate synchronic powers.

It follows that, contra Jaworski, the substantial form of a substance should not be identified with a 'structure' in which the lowest-level parts to get 'structured' are physical entities with the same force-generating powers they possessed in the wild (that is, prior to being structured). Koons offers a *transformative* hylomorphism, in which the powers of every part of a substance are replaced (so to speak)[51] by numerically distinct powers which are grounded in the nature of the substance. Since the concept of structure *presupposes* the properties of the parts which play a role within the structure, it cannot *explain* the transformation of those parts. Yet it is this transformation, in my view, which takes the sting from Kim's causal exclusion problem: the indeterminate powers of the lower-level parts of a substance, considered apart from the substance, are *never* sufficient for determining the facts about where the matter ends up.[52]

In the second place, a fundamental dualism of microscopic and macroscopic entities is averted because a substance and its accidents only *persist* in existence through the past 'cooperation' of its parts. In this version of hylomorphism, the parts of the substance are caught up within a process through which the whole substance is sustained through time, along with all of its accidental and emergent properties. Although the existence and nature of each integral part of a substance at any point in time t is constitutively grounded in the substantial form and (thereby) in the whole substance, it is suggested that they could nonetheless be contributing causes to the *later* existence of that same substance.[53] According to Koons, some portion of matter x is a *sustaining instrument* of a substance y at some moment of time t just in case x is an instrument of y at t, and there is some process P and some interval of time $[t_0, t]$ such that: (i) x is a participant in P throughout the interval $[t_0, t]$, and (ii) the existence of y at t is wholly grounded in the persistence of P in the interval $[t_0, t]$ (Koons, 2014, p. 172).

---

[51] Talk of 'replacement' here is somewhat metaphorical, since these integral parts do not survive a substantial change. The metaphor involves comparing the integral parts of a substance, such as an organism, with substances in the inorganic world that have the same physico-chemical composition.

[52] Indeed, the 'particles' of contemporary particle physics may not be substances at all, but integral parts of substances (see Table 3). It has been suggested that the fundamental physical substances are 'thermal substances' (Koons, 2019; Simpson, 2021b). According to the view put forward in Koons (2021b) and Simpson (2021b), there are, in addition, chemical substances which have thermal substances as potential parts, and biological substances with chemical substances as potential parts.

[53] Adapting the theory of immanent causation proposed in Zimmerman (1997).

Koons's hylomorphism thus introduces a diachronic, bottom-up dependency relation between the whole and its parts, in which the parts are said to 'sustain' the existence of the whole. Since the synchronic dependency is top-down, with the powers of parts grounded in the powers of the whole, whilst the diachronic dependency is bottom-up, with the later existence of the whole dependent on the earlier cooperation of its parts, there is no vicious circularity in this account of emergence. Yet the *process* in which the parts are said to cooperate in sustaining the existence of the whole must be more than the sum of its instantaneous parts, if the properties of the whole that 'emerge' through this process are to be irreducible to the synchronic properties of its parts. What kind of process could be more than the sum of its temporal parts?

Consider, for example, a collection of billiard balls ricocheting on a billiards table. The motion of the billiard balls involves numerous collisions in which the balls exercise their causal powers to change each other's momentum, and it can be understood in terms of the momenta the balls happen to have on the occasions of their separate collisions. This 'process' is nothing more than the sum of its temporal parts. The process of building a house, however, is a *teleological* process that is irreducible to the sum of its temporal parts, since it is necessary to invoke the *goal* of building the house in order to explain the ordering and occurrence of its temporal parts. For a hylomorphist like Koons, I suggest, the process which sustains a substance in existence must be more like the process of building a house than the collisions between billiard balls, since the exercise of any power of the parts is meant to contribute to the natural *end* of the whole.

Yet the process which sustains a substantial whole, such as a biological organism, must be a *natural* rather than an artificial process, in which the end of the process is not fixed by something extrinsic to the substance (like a builder) but by something intrinsic to the substance (its substantial form). It seems that in order to secure a real distinction between living organisms and heaps of matter, without falling into dualism or polite materialism, the hylomorphist should be committed to the existence of *teleology* in biology. If hylomorphism presupposes something as apparently discredited as teleology, is there room for a hylomorphic theory of substance in the philosophy of biology?

4 What Hylomorphism Means for Biology

Of the two constituent-based hylomorphic theories that I examined in Section 3 – namely, Jaworski's structural hylomorphism and Koons's transformative hylomorphism – only the *transformative* version seemed to be able to avoid the causal exclusion problem. In this section, I shall argue that, of the two transformative hylomorphic theories that I introduced in Section 2 – namely,

Marmodoro's concept-based hylomorphism and Koons's constituent-based hylomorphism – only the *constituent-based* version can provide an account of the distinctive nature of living organisms.[54] It is able to do so, I argue, because it provides a fundamental basis for the immanent, non-intentional form of teleology that features in the identity conditions of biological systems. I conclude by considering whether hylomorphism is compatible with evolution.

What Is the Nature of Biological Functions?   Teleology is the study of the relationship between things and their ends, goals or purposes, where the things in question may be entities or activities. Whilst it is uncontroversial that human activities (such as building) and artifacts (such as houses) may be said to have 'purposes', it is often supposed among philosophers that teleological thinking has been successfully evicted from modern biology. Indeed, it is widely held that the theory of evolution was the final nail in its coffin, as far as the life sciences are concerned. Nonetheless, teleology plays a significant role in carving the subject matter of biology. According to Georg Toepfer, 'teleology is closely connected to the concept of the organism and therefore has its most fundamental role in the very *definition* of biology as a particular science of natural objects' (Toepfer, 2012, p. 113, emphasis added).

Imagine a seal galumphing along the seashore. Whilst the undulating motion of its spindle-shaped body is comically clumsy, a marine biologist would consider it to be normal behaviour for a seal that is trying to move on land, being a by-product of a system of locomotion whose primary and proper function is to enable swimming under water, which is where seals commonly find their food. As Karen Neander points out, however, the notion of 'proper function' in biology has two significant and rather puzzling features (Neander, 1991b). In the first place, it appears to be a *normative* notion, in as much as there is a standard of proper functioning from which actual biological traits may diverge. For instance, if an orca rips off part of a seal's flipper in an act of predation, the damaged limb of the unfortunate pinniped does not cease thereby to be a flipper. In the second place, it appears to be a *teleological* notion, in as much as the proper function of the flippers is to steer and propel the animal under water. In other words, aquatic motion seems to be what flippers are *for*.

One of the reasons that teleological explanations are often seen to be 'unscientific' by modern philosophers is that they are forward-looking explanations that explain the means by the ends, whereas in typical scientific explanations the explanans refer to causes that are temporally *prior* to the explananda. In

---

[54] For a more positive appraisal of structural hylomorphism, which argues for its compatibility with the philosophy of biology of the New Mechanists, see De Haan (2017).

the case of artifacts, the problem is superficial. On the one hand, to say that the house has a roof because it keeps off the rain is to explain the existence of something by citing one of its effects. On the other hand, the explanans may be considered to refer implicitly to an intention shared by the architect and the builder which is prior to the explananda – namely, their *desire* that the house they are responsible for constructing should successfully keep out the rain.

The problem is more perplexing for the case of biological functions, however, in which we have no recourse to the intentions of an architect or builder who is responsible for the construction of the biological entity in question (barring some kind of Creationism). Yet the fact that the seal's flippers have the *function* of enabling it to swim underwater does seem to *explain* why it has limbs which are short and webbed, and it is rather implausible that biologists who engage in such kinds of explanation are being irrational or unscientific. Furthermore, there is no obvious way of dispensing with teleological functions in modern biology, since they have essential roles to play in identifying its subject matter.

In the first place, many biological traits are *individuated* according to their teleological function, rather than according to their morophological structure. The flippers of seals, for example, differ structurally from those of dolphins, yet both appendages play a functional role in enabling aquatic motion. In the second place, teleological functions play an important role in the *functional analysis* of a biological system, which is concerned with describing what happens when an organism functions normally (or abnormally). In the functional analysis of the human circulatory system, for example, the system is decomposed into parts which are functionally individuated (such as the heart, the arteries, etc.), which are in turn decomposed into functionally individuated parts (the atria, the ventricles, etc.), and so on, down to the cellular level (and beyond).

According to Toepfer, 'Most biological objects do not even exist as definite entities apart from the teleological perspective' (Toepfer, 2012, p. 118), which specifies a system as a subject of biological inquiry by fixing the functional roles of its parts. Indeed, 'the period of existence of an organism is not determined by the conservation of its matter. . . but by the preservation of the cycle of its activities. As the unity of this cycle is given by relating functional processes to each other, teleology plays a synthetic role for biology and has ontological consequences. The identity conditions of biological systems are given by functional analysis, not by chemical or physical descriptions' (Toepfer, 2012). Yet to conceptualise biological traits in terms of their functional ends is not to explain them in terms of their prior *causes*, which is how scientific explanations are typically supposed to operate, but rather to identify them in terms of their *effects* (Quarfood, 2006; Toepfer, 2008, 2012). How, then, should we account for the functionality of living things, which seems to set them apart in the world from other things as *biological* subjects, without invoking a purposive form of explanation that refers implicitly to the intentions of an external agent?

How Do Biological Functions Fit into the Physical World? Several proposals for 'physicalising' biological functions by situating teleologically identified explananda within the causal structure of the world have been put forward by various philosophers. According to Cummins (1976), for example, biological functions should be conceived as *causal contributions* to overall activities of the containing organism, and as being relative to our explanatory interests, since both the boundaries of the containing system and the overall activities that we may happen to be focussed upon will vary according to our concerns. Alternatively, according to Bigelow and Pargetter (1987), a biological characteristic has a function if it has a *disposition* that is apt for natural selection, or if it systematically enhances the survival of an organism within the context of its natural habitat.

Causal role functions have featured heavily in the philosophy of mind, where philosophers have sought to physicalise psychological states by expressing them in terms of functionalist theories. David Lewis's functionalist philosophy of mind arose out of the rubble of philosophical behaviourism in the 1960s, which had sought to reduce mental phenomena to physical dispositions. Whilst abandoning the attempt to define psychological properties explicitly in terms of physical dispositions, the functionalist project aimed to show how they could remain anchored in the physical world by being defined in terms of the *functional role* that they play in a physical theory. For Lewis, it is Ramsey sentences which best explicate the functional definitions that this project requires (Lewis, 1970). Lewis's recipe for functionalising the mind consisted of two stages.

First, suppose we are seeking a theory of some property in terms of something we take to be better understood or with which we are at least more familiar. Let us distinguish between the familiar terms O and the new terms P for which we are seeking an analysis. Suppose O consists of predicates describing overt physical behaviour and P describes psychological states. Suppose also that we have a theory T that consists of a single sentence, $P(c) \rightarrow O(c)$, for some constant c. T may be understood as saying that $O(c)$ obtains whenever $P(c)$ obtains. The theory T, at this stage, is parameterised by both psychological terms $P(c)$ and behavioural terms $O(c)$, that is, $T(P(c), O(c))$.

According to Lewis's account, the P-terms 'stand in specified causal (and other) relations to entities named by O-terms, and to one another' (Lewis, 1972,

p. 253). To form the Ramsey sentence, we replace the P terms with variables over which the sentence is said to quantify: $\exists x(x(c) \rightarrow O(c))$. We should read the resulting sentence, $\exists x T[x(c), O(c)]$, which is meant to capture the factual content of the original theory, as saying that there are some fundamental relations such that $T[x(c), O(c)]$ is satisfied when the variables $x(c)$ in the Ramsey sentence are assigned these relations.

Second, Lewis offers a way of identifying the referents of functionally defined terms whose causal roles we assign a priori, such as psychological terms like desires and beliefs, by identifying them with the physical occupants of their roles that scientists discover a posteriori. Having obtained the Ramsey sentence for a psychological theory involving desires and beliefs, we are at liberty to settle the metaphysics of what underlies our 'folk psychology' by reflecting upon the description of the world offered by our best physics. As Menzies and Price put it: 'The core of the second stage. . . is that what the first stage provides, in effect, is a non-trivial target for empirical investigation: in this case, investigation of what it is, in fact, that plays the causal role' (Menzies & Price, 2008, p. 6).

Functionalism looks like a promising strategy for physicalising life and accounting for the functionality of living things without reifying their teleology, if we assume that the physical building blocks of nature and their activities can be described without teleology. It begins with whatever scientists believe to be the true biological theory that captures whichever pattern of physical interactions is deemed definitive of life, and then replaces the biological terms with variables which stand for those physical entities and physical states which realise the relevant pattern. The resulting functionalist model is expressed partly in the language of fundamental physics, in which the inputs and outputs to the system must be described, as well as the topic-neutral language of causation, dispositions, and conditionals (plus terms from logic and mathematics), in order to express how the truth claims of the less fundamental biological theory are ultimately realised in the model of the more fundamental physical theory.

A crucial question arises, however, concerning how to interpret the clauses of the Ramsey sentence (Koons & Pruss, 2017). There is more than one way of doing so. If such a clause were conceived as an indicative conditional, for instance, it might say: (1) if the system x *is* in internal state S_n and in input state I_m at time t, then x [with probability r] *is* in internal state S_k and output state O_j at the next relevant time $t + \delta t$ (p. 195). If such a clause were conceived as a subjunctive conditional, it might say: (2) if the system x *were* in internal state S_n and in input state I_m at time t, then x *would* [with probability r] be in internal state S_k and output state O_j at the next relevant time $t + \delta t$ (Koons & Pruss, 2017).

Some of the standard problems with conditional accounts of dispositions, which prompted the turn to powers in contemporary metaphysics (Section 1), arise again here. Koons and Pruss ask us to imagine the case of an individual – 'the system x' – who has an explosive belt strapped to her. This belt will detonate if the system x is in internal state S_n and receives input I_m at time t. Once she puts on this belt, both conditionals (1) and (2) are rendered false, even though the bomb never in fact goes off, and so the Ramsey sentence for the biological theory which contains these clauses is falsified. Yet donning an explosive belt, however unwise, does not make it untrue that someone is *alive*. We might of course attempt to restrict the context in which these conditionals are evaluated, by insisting that only causal factors that are internal to the biological system x are relevant. Yet we can easily rework the example so that it refers to a fatal disease rather than a dangerous personal accessory, in order to undermine the relevance of the distinction between internal and external causal factors.

Koons and Pruss also consider the possibility of strengthening the antecedents of conditionals (1) and (2) to include the claim that the whole system survives until the next relevant time $t + \delta t$. However, as they point out, such a revision also runs into difficulties. Adapting a thought-experiment put forward by Harry Frankfurt (Frankfurt, 1969), they imagine a hypothetical manipulator who wants the biological system in question to follow a certain rigidly defined script throughout the course of its 'life'. If the system were to show signs of deviating from the micro-managing script that has been contrived for it, then the manipulator would intervene internally, causing the system to continue acting in accordance with the script. If the script specifies that at time $t + \delta t$ the biological system is to be in state S_n, for example, then that is what would happen, regardless of what state the biological system were to occupy at time t.

Frankfurt used this thought-experiment to cast doubt on the claim that freedom of the will requires the existence of alternative possibilities. It seems obvious that the mere *presence* of a manipulator – who never actually intervenes in the operations of the agent – cannot deprive the agent of its free will, and yet the mere presence of such a manipulator *is* sufficient to undermine any alternative possibilities. Koons and Pruss use the same thought-experiment to cast doubt on the claim that the existence of biological states depends on the truth of conditionals which link states to inputs, outputs, and each other, and hence to undermine any interpretation of the clauses of the Ramsey sentence in terms of indicative or subjunctive conditionals. Again, it seems obvious that the mere presence of the manipulator cannot deprive a biological system of its biological states, and yet its mere presence is sufficient to falsify conditionals which causally link its biological states, such as clauses (1) or (2).

The problem with interpreting the clauses of a Ramsey sentence in terms of indicative or subjunctive conditionals, like (1) and (2), is that they offer *descriptive* rather than *normative* analyses. Such an interpretation of functionalism attempts to anchor the functional role of a biological trait in terms of a subset of its actual causal roles. The proper function of a biological trait, however, is not necessarily something it *actually* does. On the one hand, disease or injury in an organism, or some unpropitious circumstance, can prevent its subsystems from performing behaviour associated with their proper functions. Most acorns do not become oak trees, for instance, since they are food for many animals and are often consumed in whole or in part. It is highly implausible that a purely descriptive theory could accommodate the possible effects of every conceivable mishap or malfunction to which a biological system might be subjected. On the other hand, what something actually does may have nothing to do with its proper function. As Neander points out, a tumour may play a causal role in a pathological process which disrupts the functions of parts of an organism – for example, by pressing on an artery to the brain – yet it does not seem correct to identify the causal role played by a tumour with its 'proper function' (Neander, 1991a, p.181). What is needed, according to Koons and Pruss, is a modified functionalist account which is able to exclude cases like the manipulator by adding a *normality condition* to the antecedents of clauses (1) or (2).

Is Normativity a Product of Evolution?   A simple way of establishing a notion of normality is to define the norm in terms of what usually occurs in a population. We might say that a biological system *normally* enters state S_m after state S_n, as a result of an input I_m to the system, provided it is *likely* to do this. Such an amendment would permit us to discount the interference of a micro-managing manipulator or a crippling disease to the functioning of an individual organism. One obvious difficulty with such an approach, however, is that serious dysfunction can become widespread throughout a population during epidemics, where large numbers of systems fail to do what they are supposed to do. Widespread malfunction can also be caused by environmental catastrophes. It seems there is more to the normative aspect of biological functions than the mere frequency of traits in a population.

A more plausible approach to the problem of normativity has been advanced by a number of etiological theories of biological functions, which broadly share the view that what counts as a function of a biological trait is determined by that trait's evolutionary history. According to Neander, who was influenced by an earlier theory put forward by Larry Wright (Wright, 1973, 1976), we should think of the function of a trait as being the effect for which that trait was selected. For example, if a heart has the proper function of pumping blood, then it is 'because pumping blood is what hearts did that caused them to be favoured by natural selection' (Neander, 1991a, p. 168). More precisely, it is 'the proper function of an item (X) of an organism (O) to do that which items of X's type did to contribute to the inclusive fitness of O's ancestors, and which caused the genotype, of which X is the phenotypic expression, to be selected by natural selection' (Neander, 1991a p. 174, where X quantifies over both evolved biological parts and biological processes). Significantly, natural selection can only operate on *past* causal contributions to inclusive fitness, and operates upon types rather than tokens. Millikan has developed a similar etiological theory independently (Millikan, 1984, 1989).

An etiological theory does not identify the biological category of a thing with its physical structure or causal dispositions. Rather, it claims that the proper function of a thing, which identifies its biological category, has to do with its evolutionary history. On the one hand, this means that something can count as a token of the relevant type even if it is malformed and unable to fulfill the causal roles that we happen to associate with being a token of that type, such as a damaged heart which is failing to pump blood. On the other hand, this means that things which can perform the causal role we associate with certain types do not necessarily count as tokens of that type. For example, artificial devices have been designed which can pump blood around the human body, but these do not count as members of the biological category 'heart'. According to Millikan, the task of an etiological theory of proper functions is to define the normative sense in which a biological entity has been 'designed' to do this, or is 'supposed' to do that, but in naturalistic and non-mysterious terms.

An etiological theory of biological function, such as Neander's or Millikan's, seeks to support the teleological aspect of biological functions. In other words, it aims to uphold the kind of 'forward-looking' explanation that is found in the biological sciences, in which the effect of biological trait (such as bestowing a capacity for aquatic motion) may be said to explain the presence of that trait (such as why seals have limbs which are webbed), even though the effect of that trait clearly *postdates* the explanandum. The teleological aspect of biological functions is properly grounded, according to these theorists, not by importing the purposes of a designer within biological processes, nor by appealing to something as exotic as backwards causation, but through an implicit, 'backward-looking' reference to the process of natural selection that *predates* the explanandum. Such an account, they maintain, is scientifically acceptable.

Nonetheless, etiological theories of biological function are subject to some serious philosophical objections. In the first place, as Koons points out, they appear to be circular: although the function of a trait is supposed to be the effect for which that type of trait was apparently favoured by natural selection, it is unclear how the *concept* of reproduction can be defined naturalistically without reference to function.[55] After all, the reproduction of a biological organism favoured by natural selection is not a matter of copying a system particle-for-particle or state-for-state. No such reproductions ever take place in biology. Rather, reproduction in biology involves the successful copying of *essential* features of the system in question, and some of these essential features will have to be specified in terms of biological functions. Yet Neander's and Millikan's accounts of biological function, as Koons observes, seem to have 'put the reproductive cart before the functional horse' (Koons, 2021a, p. 13).

A second objection follows on the heels of the first. Since a biological trait can never be 'normal' in the generation in which it first appears, because the normative aspect of its biological function is supposed to derive from the reproductive history of that trait, it follows that the first system to emerge with the capacity for self-reproduction – and whatever other traits are deemed to be definitive of life – could not itself have been a 'living' entity.

Neander considers the hypothetical possibility of a creature which 'freakishly coalesced into existence one day, without evolution or design. . . Surely, we can correctly ascribe biological functions to any such complex, intricately integrated organisms, despite their lack of history and accidental genesis' (Neander, 1991a, p. 169). Her response to such hypothetical examples of spontaneously generated lifeforms is to deny that we have any reliable intuitions that can be brought to bear in such cases, and to double down on her etiological theory: 'I contend that we could not reliably place them in any category until we knew or could infer the things' history' (p. 180).

There is more at stake, however, than the problem of how to tie labels to hypothetical monsters. If biological traits are individuated according to their biological function, and if new traits which causally contribute to the survival of an organism have no biological function when first they appear in its evolutionary history, then we must conclude that such traits are epiphenomenal qua *biological* traits. Yet if biological entities have no causal powers in virtue of having biological properties – such as the property of being alive – then the biological properties which individuate these composite entities are subject to

---

[55] A similar objection is made by Bence Nanay in Nanay (2010). He observes that the etiological view grounds functional ascriptions on trait types which were favoured in the past by natural selection, and yet trait types are often individuated by their functionality. He concludes: '... the etiological theory of function cannot stand, for it has to rely on an independent account of individuating trait types, and no such account is available for the etiological theory' (p. 419).

Kim's causal exclusion problem. In that case, we have good reason to drop such entities from our ontology (see Section 3).

Pruss has formulated a third objection which, rather than focussing on the first appearance of traits that are favoured by natural selection, proposes a possible world in which natural selection is prevented from performing its usual role in biology. We are to imagine a duplicate of Earth in which every organism at the moment of death is transported – by rather sophisticated, biophilic aliens – to a separate, causally isolated universe where it is able to continue its life interminably, reproducing itself to a maximal degree. In such a hospitable multiverse, which Pruss has christened 'the Great Grazing Ground', natural selection would be unable to operate, even though all the organisms on Earth would be just as they are in the actual world (Koons & Pruss, 2017).[56]

We can see this is the case if we conceive the explanatory role of natural selection as embodying a form of contrastive explanation. According to Sober, natural selection explains why a population consists of organisms which have *these* biological traits rather than *those* biological traits. Likewise, we can understand how a biological trait could causally contribute to an instance of survival or reproduction if we conceive this particular trait as featuring in a contrastive explanation of why *this* instance of survival or reproduction took place instead of not taking place. In the duplicate Earth proposed in Pruss's thought-experiment, however, every organism succeeds in reproducing itself, so natural selection has no role to play in a contrastive explanation of why a population has *these* traits rather than *those*.

It follows that Neander's and Millikan's definitions of biological normativity, which depend on the operation of natural selection, have no application to the duplicate Earth in Pruss's thought-experiment. Consequently, they must conclude that there is no life on this duplicate of the Earth. And yet the causal history of the physical properties of this duplicate is identical to the causal history of the physical properties of our Earth. The only difference between them is that an organism on the duplicate Earth has a history that continues within another region of the Great Grazing Ground that is causally isolated from duplicate Earth. This will not do. It is highly implausible that the facts about whether or not there is life on the duplicate Earth should depend on causally unconnected events occurring in other parts of the Great Grazing Ground.

More recently, Pruss has put forward another Frankfurt-inspired thought experiment that counts against Neander's and Millikan's definitions of biological normativity, which I shall christen the case of the Counterfactual

---

[56] Blog: https://alexanderpruss.blogspot.com/2009/03/evolutionary-theories-of-mind.html.

Custodian.[57] We are to imagine a duplicate of our Earth, once again, which has a biological history just like ours. The difference is that this duplicate is overseen by a powerful custodian who plays a role like Frankfurt's counterfactual intervener. The custodian has a script for all the details of the biological history of this planet, and if there is any deviation from this script, the custodian will intervene to restore the same biological conditions that would have obtained had there been no deviations. Specifically, the custodian will act in such a way as to prevent there from being any deviation from the script in the reproduction or survival of any lifeforms on this duplicate of Earth. As it happens, the script for the duplicate of the Earth matches exactly the history of life on Earth, and by good fortune, no intervention by the custodian is ever required.

Yet it seems that Neander and Millikan must deny that there is any life on this duplicate Earth. The crucial thought in these evolutionary accounts of normativity is that the proper function of some trait simply denotes its contribution towards the survival of a reproductively established family. Yet many of the counterfactuals which are supposed to define proper function, according to the etiological account, fail to hold on this duplicate of the Earth. Pruss considers the case of a bird on Earth being attacked by a predator, where the bird escapes by flying and subsequently reproduces. The wings of this organism contribute to the survival of the organism on Earth. On the duplicate of the Earth, however, had the bird failed to fly, the custodian would have intervened by moving the bird out of danger. The custodian would then have restored the same biological conditions that would have obtained had there been no deviations from the script. As it happens, no such interventions occur, so both the Earth and its duplicate share the same history. The only difference is that the duplicate is being watched by the custodian. Yet it is deeply implausible that the mere presence of this passive custodian is sufficient to undermine the proper functions of every organism in this duplicate of the Earth.

Some philosophers of science, no doubt, will have a deep-seated aversion to modifying their views about evolutionary accounts of normativity on the basis of such highly contrived scenarios as the Great Grazing Ground or the Counterfactual Custodian. My first two objections, they should recall, were concerned rather with worries about circularity and epiphenomenalism. Yet if one is moved by Frankfurt-inspired examples to add a normality condition to functionalism, then it seems one should be moved by the same logic to reject an etiological account of normativity. And if one is seeking a *theoretical definition* of a function which carves nature at its joints, such definitions must apply

---

[57] Blog: https://alexanderpruss.blogspot.com/2021/10/another-problem-with-evolutionary.html

even in highly contrived scenarios.[58] What Pruss's hypothetical examples usefully highlight, I think, is how Neander's and Millikan's accounts of biological teleology fail to embody the kind of *immanent* teleology that is needed.

How Does Hylomorphism Explain Normativity? According to Koons and Pruss, we do not have to abandon the functionalist project in order to accommodate the normative and teleological aspects of biological functions. Rather, we can achieve this integration by interpreting the clauses of the Ramsey sentence that explicates the functional definitions of biology in terms of *powers*. Specifically, we should say that: system x's being in internal state S_n confers upon it the *causal power* to produce output state O_j and internal state S_k immediately in response to input state I_m (Koons & Pruss, 2017). Powers have teleology built into their very definitions, since they are fundamentally *directed* towards certain manifestations. In this powerist solution to the problem of normativity, a biological substance may thus be supposed (in a normative sense) to produce manifestation E on occasions of C just in case it is in the nature of the biological substance in question to include a C-to-E power. As we shall see, however, the viability of this solution depends on how we construe the notion of a *nature* and its relation to something's *powers*.

Like the etiological theorist, the contemporary powerist avoids appealing to the purposes of a designer or to backwards causation in order to ground the teleological aspect of biological functions, invoking an implicit, backwards-looking reference to the real and irreducible *potentials* of something, which predate the actual activities in which it is engaged. The powerist approach also has the advantage of avoiding the circularity objection directed against etiological theories. Since the normative aspect of a biological function does not derive from the role it has played in natural selection, but from the inherently powerful nature of the entity which exemplifies the associated biological trait, there is no circularity in specifying successful instances of reproduction in terms of biological functions. Likewise, by supplying a source of immanent teleology within nature, the powerist circumvents the Great Grazing Ground and the Counterfactual Custodian objections. The facts about whether or not certain things are alive or have biological functions do not depend upon causally unconnected events elsewhere or whether or not they are being observed by something that might have interfered with them had they behaved differently.

To overcome worries about epiphenomenalism, however, it is not sufficient merely to introduce powers into the ontology. Biological teleology requires *both* a powers metaphysics *and* the existence of causal powers at the level of

---

[58] After all, in this discussion we have been seeking a realist account of biological entities.

biological entities; that is, it demands an ontology in which a biological organism may be attributed powers as a macroscopic, *biological* entity. As I argued in Section 3, a transformative hylomorphism, in which the powers of the microscopic parts of a substance are made to depend upon the substance as a whole, is able to overcome Kim's causal exclusion objection against 'higher-level' powers. In my discussion of this problem, I focussed on Koons's constituent-based version of hylomorphism. However, Marmodoro's principle-based hylomorphism (see Section 2) is not obviously subject to Kim's causal exclusion problem either, and also affirms the existence of biological substances with irreducible powers.

Yet Koons's constituent-based hylomorphism and Marmodoro's principle-based hylomorphism differ radically in how they construe the *nature* of a biological substance and the relation between something's nature and its powers. According to Koons, the substantial form of a substance plays a fundamental role in *grounding* a substance's causal powers. To the extent that we take Koons to be following Aquinas, this grounding relation cannot be conceived as strict logical entailment. For Aquinas, there is supposed to be some 'metaphysical distance', so to speak, between the substantial form of a particular substance and the causal powers it exemplifies, which is properly expressed by the scholastic distinction between the *essence* of something and its *propria*. In scholastic metaphysics, a thing is attributed propria as well as accidents, where its propria (like its accidents) are characteristics which are not part of the definition of the thing and are not logically entailed by its essence, but which (unlike its accidents) are said nonetheless to 'flow' from its essence.

An oft-cited example is the property of risibility. It is not part of the *definition* of being human that one necessarily laughs in humorous circumstances, nor is it the case that someone who persistently fails to exemplify this property is disqualified from being human. However, risibility is deemed to be part of the propria of a human being, since it is a capacity that is widely exercised by human beings in humorous circumstances. Unlike the accidental property, say, of having purple hair, it is perceived as reflecting something of the nature of a human being as a *rational animal*.

The claim, then, that 'human beings normally laugh in humorous circumstances' is not an empirical generalisation that is falsified by a single counterexample, nor is it merely a statistical generalisation which lacks any modal force. Rather, the propria of a human being *necessarily* belong to what it is to be human, without necessarily belonging to an individual human being.[59] To put it more formally, the logic of propria is not captured by the claim: if *F* is

---

[59] See Thompson's account of 'Aristotelian categoricals' in Thompson (2008, chp. 4).

in the propria of O, then, necessarily, an x of type O has the property F. Rather, we should say: if F is in the propria of O, then, necessarily, *some* x's of type O have the property F. At least that is how propria are often understood.

From Aquinas's perspective, many features that modern essentialists associate with the natures of things should be classified as propria rather than parts of their essences. The modern empiricist who identifies the essence of something with a set of properties it supposedly exemplifies in all possible worlds sets the bar too high for biological essentialism. The danger of rejecting the distinction between something's essence and its propria is that one is likely to end up a biological eliminativist, having despaired of identifying a set of necessary and sufficient properties for something to count as a biological entity of a certain kind. Aquinas is more realistic, recognising that, whilst the natures of things cannot be known a priori but must be abstracted from our experience of many exemplars, an individual exemplar may fail to live up to its nature in certain respects. Where a characteristic that is part of the propria of something is missing in an individual, one is entitled to seek an explanation of why that is the case. The agelast may have been stunted in their early development or scarred by psychological abuse.

The distinction is relevant to one of Neander's objections to the 'propensity theory' put forward by Bigelow and Pargetter (Bigelow & Pargetter, 1987), which identifies biological functions with dispositions that contribute to a creature's survival.[60] As Neander observes, biological traits which have functions in common do not always have dispositions in common. She gives the example of an atrophied thyroid gland, which has the function of producing thyroid hormones in appropriate quantities, like that of a normal thyorid gland, but lacks the disposition to perform this function because it has atrophied (Neander, 1991b, p. 466, fn. 13). Indeed, dysfunctional traits are thought to be dysfunctional precisely because they have functions that they are supposed to perform but they lack the actual dispositions that are necessary to perform them.

Powerists who adopt Koons's constituent-based theory of hylomorphism, in which matter and form are metaphysical constituents of a substance, can offer an account of a biological substance in which certain powers are in the *nature* of the substance without necessarily being instantiated in the individual substance. To do so, I suggest, they will have to allow that the substantial form of a substance can be realised in the activity of a substance to varying degrees. One way to express this thought in terms of matter and form is to say that the

---

[60] This distinction is also key to how Oderberg (2007), Dumsday (2012), and other neo-Aristotelians distinguish the biological species of evolutionary biologists from hylomorphic species.

matter of some substances may be *more unified* by their substantial forms than the matter of other substances of the same nature.

In Marmodoro's principle-based hylomorphism, however, there can be no recourse to the metaphysical distance between the substantial form of a substance and the powers it exemplifies or to degrees of unity within a substance, since the substantial form is not the *cause* of the substance having those powers but is merely the *principle* by which certain 'power-tropes' that are ontologically prior to the substance get to be re-identified as the powers of a substance. In Marmodoro's account of the nature of substance, matter and form are not metaphysical constituents but are abstractions from something constructed according to our explanatory interests. We cannot therefore appeal to her transformative theory of hylomorphism to provide an objective basis for the immanent, non-intentional form of teleology that features in the identity conditions of biological systems. For this, we need something more like Koons's theory of hylomorphism, which is both transformative and constituent-based.

Is Hylomorphism Inconsistent with Evolution?   Perhaps the greatest obstacle to rehabilitating Aristotle's ancient doctrine of hylomorphism and applying it to problems in contemporary philosophy is the perceived incompatibility of Aristotelian essentialism with the modern theory of evolution. In the first place, doesn't hylomorphism presuppose the *fixity* of biological species – contrary to the theory of evolution, which explains how species change over time? In the second place, haven't the properties of individuals (and hence their natures) been rendered redundant in explaining the diversity of biological forms, since the theory of evolution conceives *populations* rather than individuals to be the units of organisation, and explains change in species in terms of the statistical properties of large ensembles of genes? Both of these objections to hylomorphism can be addressed, I suggest, if we are careful to avoid some common pitfalls in the interpretation of Aristotelian essentialism.

As Walsh observes (Walsh, 2020), the first of these anti-essentialist arguments targets *typological* forms of essentialism, which define a species in terms of a canonical set of unchanging physical properties that are supposed to constitute the essence of a member of that species. It is now widely recognised, however, that Aristotelian essentialism is not a typological form of essentialism (Balme, 1987; Pellegrin, 1987) but a *teleological* form of essentialism (Lennox, 1987, p. 340, fn. 4), in which natures play a teleological role in explaining why organisms have certain biological traits which resemble one another. In applying the theory of hylomorphism to contemporary biology, I suggest, hylomorphists need not require natural kinds to be united by the common possession of any timeless and structurally identical features, though they should require the substantial forms of biological substances to impose certain *constraints* on the phenotypes of organisms which share the same nature.[61]

The second argument targets essentialism in general by mobilising the anti-individualism inherent within the 'modern evolutionary synthesis'. According to Elliott Sober, the great watershed in modern biology achieved by Darwin was the redirection of the explanandum from properties of *individual* organisms to properties of *populations* (Sober, 1980). As Margaret Morrison puts it: 'one needed only general statistical laws about the interactions among individuals, rather than specific knowledge of the individuals themselves, in order to determine the effects of evolutionary mechanisms' (Morrison, 2000, p. 215). The source of change in a population responsible for driving these evolutionary mechanisms is random genetic mutation, which is thought to have nothing to do with the natures of individual organisms. The population is treated as an entity which is subject to its own forces and obeys its own laws, whilst the properties of an individual organism are regarded as being just as 'peripheral' to evolutionary theory as the properties of a single molecule to the kinetic theory of gases (Sober, 1980, p. 370). In Sober's estimation, 'essentialism lost its grip when populations came to be thought of as real' (p. 381).

As Walsh argues, however, whilst the modern evolutionary synthesis abstracts away from individual organisms and their capacities, 'developmental biology shows that one must appeal to the capacities of organisms to explain what makes adaptive evolution *adaptive*' (Walsh, 2020, p. 425, emphasis added). Ironically, he points out, 'the specific capacities in question are precisely those that ... constitute the nature of an organism' (Walsh, 2020). It is these intrinsic capacities of the organism which ensure that the phenotypic variation upon which natural selection operates is in fact a *non-random* subset of all the possible phenotypes that could be generated, in order to preserve the well functioning of the organism.

A central concept in what is now commonly called the 'extended' evolutionary synthesis (as opposed to the 'modern' evolutionary synthesis) is the notion of *phenotypic plasticity*, which 'consists in an organism's finely tuned capacity to develop and maintain a viable, stable homeostatic end state that is typical for organisms of its kind by the implementation of compensatory changes to its behaviour, structure and physiology' (Walsh, 2020, pp. 440–1). The developmental systems which realise the phenotypic plasticity of the organism, whilst

---

[61] Christopher Austin has constructed a neo-Aristotelian theory of biological natural kinds, in which the essence of a natural kind to which an organism belongs consist of dispositional properties realised by its development modules that support different 'morphological profiles' (Austin, 2018).

robust against deleterious change, achieve their robustness by responding with compensatory changes that underwrite the mutability of the organism. Since an organism has the capacity to attain its end state by pursuing many different developmental trajectories, the nature that grounds this capacity must be associated with a 'phenotypic repertoire' that is far wider than any canonical set of unchanging properties (West-Eberhard, 2003, p. 146).

In applying the theory of hylomorphism to the theory of evolution, I conclude, hylomorphists should not ally themselves to the modern evolutionary synthesis, in which changes in the individual phenotype are the causal consequences of changes within a population, but to the extended evolutionary synthesis, in which changes in gene frequencies within a population may be mediated by the natures of individual organisms. Indeed, the hylomorphist is able to give an account of a biological organism's intrinsic nature in terms of a substance which is metaphysically composed of matter and substantial form.[62]

Hylomorphism, I believe, does not run into any serious difficulties in admitting variations with respect to biological species as part of a natural evolutionary process. Yet in distinguishing *biological* species, which are defined in a plurality of ways by evolutionary biologists, from *metaphysical* species, which are supposed to share the same nature, hylomorphists may encounter a problem: changes in biological species are typically thought to be small and are often supposed to be continuous, but changes in metaphysical species are often thought to be large and are necessarily discontinuous. Where do the boundaries between metaphysical species fall? Many hylomorphists would wish to distinguish the substantial forms of animals from the substantial forms of plants on the basis of their higher-level brain functions, for instance. Should hylomorphists admit that, all living things – including animals, plants, and human beings – may ultimately belong to a *single* metaphysical species? In other words, given the evidence of evolution, should they think of biological substances as all having the same type of substantial form?

Although hylomorphists must distinguish the concept of *metaphysical* species from the various notions of *biological* species typically used by evolutionary biologists, a biologically informed hylomorphist will be sensitive, I suggest, to discontinuities in evolutionary development, such as periods of relative stability followed by bursts of change. Stephen Jay Gould's and Niles Eldredge's theory of 'punctuated equilibria', for example, which claims that populations show little morphological change for most of their geological history punctuated by rapid and rare speciation events (Eldredge & Gould, 1989), might

---

[62] For a recent defence of intrinsic biological essentialism, see Dumsday (2012). For a briefer defence in connection with natural law theory, see Angier (2021, Section 4.2).

submit to a hylomorphic interpretation that brings biological and metaphysical notions of species closer together. If a hylomorphist were to develop this proposal, the successive and stable equilibria points in Gould's theory of evolution might be taken to represent metaphysical species, whilst the short-lived transitional populations might be supposed to represent substantial forms that fail to belong to a species (or a kind of mixture of two species with each member close to the borderline with the other).[63] In this halting, non-gradualist picture of evolutionary development, substantial forms could be given a role in grounding the specific biological adaptations of each organism. Of course, this is just a thought-provoking conjecture that requires further development.

There is a deeper ontological issue that needs to be addressed. Living organisms, unbeknownst to Aristotle, are relative latecomers in the history of the cosmos, yet they are not of the same metaphysical species as the chemical compounds that preceded them.[64] How are such ontological transitions in history supposed to be accounted for in terms of those substances and powers extant within nature *prior* to their occurrence? It was a widely accepted principle among classical and medieval philosophers that causes must be commensurate with their effects, inasmuch as a cause must, in some sense, *contain* what is required to produce its effect. Ontological transitions in the history of the cosmos, however, such as the emergence of life from non-life, would seem to involve causes conferring upon their effects significantly new, causally powerful features that they themselves lack. Must hylomorphists regard such transitions as entirely mysterious, or novel substantial forms as being created ex nihilo?

Perhaps part of the trouble, if trouble there be,[65] arises from the assumption that large-scale substances – like plants – emerged from small-scale substances – like molecules – by a process of ontological *fusion* (or 'ontological aggregation'), in which small-scale substances somehow conspired to generate large-scale substances. Koons has suggested the opposite might be the case: the cosmos may have begun as a single substance that has been undergoing a process of ontological *fission* (or, 'ontological disaggregation') into smaller substances, starting with 'proto-clusters, then galaxies, then stars and planetary systems, then proto-ecological systems with inherent features of a convective and thermal nature, then biotic systems consisting of populations of identical

---

[63] This interpretation of 'monsters' was suggested to me by Koons in correspondence.

[64] After all, this discussion has been in pursuit of a hylomorphic account of the unity of a biological entity which can offer a real and objective distinction between a living organism and a mere aggregate of physical stuff (or a mere collection of chemicals).

[65] See Boulter (2021) for a neo-Aristotelian perspective on the 'principle of proportionality', which seeks to obviate any difficulties it might seem to present to these ontological transitions.

one-celled organisms, and finally individual multicellular organisms' (Koons, 2018, p. 384).

This alternative picture of cosmic evolution may be motivated by the idea that the cosmos began as a single quantum system – a soup of ephemeral particles and cosmic radiation – in which the properties of any subsystem depended on the quantum state of the total system. A hylomorphic account of cosmology that begins with a single substance, I suggest, will be sensitive to any discontinuities in its temporal development that may correspond to fission events, such as the occurrence of spontaneous symmetry breaking, as well as continuities in physical systems that may correspond to the presence of substantial forms, such as the persistence of chemical forms (Koons, 2019; Simpson, 2021b). A hylomorphist has reason to be sceptical about the possibility of achieving a 'theory of everything' in terms of the continuous development of a single physical system. The behaviour of everything in the early cosmos may have been describable solely in terms of a single physical theory, but one might reasonably doubt whether this remains so for the messy world in which we find ourselves. Rather, there is a 'dappledness' to nature's laws which seems to demand a plurality of theories and practices in order to discover what things the world contains and investigate their causal powers (Cartwright, 1999).

If hylomorphists were to build on the metaphysical proposal that the world began as a single substance which underwent ontological fission, they might think of this primordial substance as *containing* the potentialities for all the other substances the world currently contains.[66] The intuitive idea is that all of these potential substances get 'unpacked' in the course of a cosmic process involving different phases of emergent complexity, in which new kinds of substances (for example, living substances) are generated at later stages which are neither reducible to nor supervene upon substances that existed at earlier stages (for example, chemical substances). All of these other substances, however, remain embedded in the cosmic substance (Dumsday, 2016). Far from being a barren void, the cosmic space in which we find ourselves situated would be a veritable 'womb of the worlds'; a substance which *always* contained the potentiality for life.[67]

Such a view will have to be squared with Aristotle's repeated claim that actuality is *prior* to potentiality. In other words, something that is already actual would be needed in order to act on all of this potency; it will never be actualised

---

[66] For a metaphysical model in which the cosmos counts as a single hylomorphic substance with a single substantial form, see Simpson (2021a, 2023).

[67] This metaphor for outer space was suggested by the scholar of Medieval and Renaissance literature, C. S. Lewis, in his celebrated science fiction novel, 'Out of the Silent Planet'.

on its own (Metaphysics XII.6 1071b13-14).[68] It may be that some hylomorphists will choose to break with Aristotle at this point by denying this principle, whereas others may abandon naturalism for a type of theistic evolution in which a divine being has a role to play in generating novel substances.[69] For my own part, I am inclined to think that, if the cosmos began as a single substance, it could have a power for *self-dividing* (like an amoeba, for example), and that such a cosmology need not involve a rejection of any of the fundamental principles of Aristotle's philosophy of nature.[70] But this conjecture is highly speculative. Clearly, there is much work to be done in adapting and applying the ancient metaphysics of hylomorphism to contemporary evolutionary theories in biology and modern cosmology. The time seems to be ripe for doing it.

5 Concluding Remarks

Aristotle's doctrine of hylomorphism is once again an area of active research and debate within mainstream analytic philosophy. Hylomorphism carves the natural world into substances which are metaphysical composites of matter and form, and seeks to explain how the parts of a composite entity can be unified such that they count as the parts of a single individual.

In Section 1, I considered how hylomorphism was displaced by a corpuscularian conception of nature, but noted how, with the rise of 'neo-Aristotelian' metaphysics and the increasing autonomy of the 'special sciences', there is the prospect for rehabilitating hylomorphism as an alternative form of naturalism to both reductive and non-reductive versions of physicalism. Many different contemporary versions of hylomorphism have been put forward, however, which have been shaped by different motivations and metaphysical commitments.

In Section 2, I put forward a classification scheme for navigating contemporary hylomorphisms, dividing them into *powerist* versus *non-powerist* approaches, according to whether they affirm a 'powers ontology' in which fundamental properties are powers; and *constituent-based* versus *concept-based* approaches, depending on whether they conceive matter and form as having a metaphysical reality that is constitutive of the physical reality of a substance independently of our conceptual schemes and activities.

---

[68] In Metaphysics XII.6, Aristotle rejects the view of 'the theologians who generate the world from night, or the natural philosophers who say that all things were together' (1071b27–29).

[69] This appears to be Tabaczek's view in Tabaczek (2023), although he thinks of substantial forms as being 'educed' from prime matter and of God's role as 'instrumentalising' their natural causes. He does not affirm the existence of a primordial cosmic substance with a power for self-dividing.

[70] It does not follow that this form of naturalism must be atheistic. The substantial forms of all these potential substances could exemplify the divine ideas of a single mind (Ward, 2020).

I identified a further layer of division in how hylomorphists think of the unity of substances, distinguishing between *structural* hylomorphists, like Jaworski, who conceive of substances as wholes whose physical parts have been related such that they fulfil certain functional roles, and *transformative* hylomorphists, like Marmodoro, who think the matter from which a substance is generated must be 'transformed' such that its parts depend upon the whole for their causal powers or identities. I noted that constituent-based hylomorphists who are structural hylomorphists have difficulties accounting for the unity of the substance, but that constituent-based hylomorphists can be transformative hylomorphists, like Koons, if they acknowledge that the powers of the parts of a substance are grounded in a single substantial form and reject a univocal conception of unity.

In Section 3, I argued that, in order for composite macroscopic entities to have irreducible powers that make a causal difference to how nature unfolds, they must have substantial forms which *transform* their matter such that the powers of their microscopic parts are made to depend on the composite entity as a whole. I argued that Jaworski's powerist, constituent-based hylomorphism, which is a structural form of hylomorphism, is subject to Kim's causal exclusion objection, as a result of its physicalised conception of matter and its structuralist conception of form. I showed how Koons's alternative powerist, constituent-based hylomorphism, which is a *transformative* version of hylomorphism, is able to avoid this problem without falling into a vitalistic form of dualism, because it grounds the synchronic powers of the microscopic parts of a substance in corresponding primary powers of the whole. Koons's version of hylomorphism is therefore able to accommodate the existence of microscopic and macroscopic substances, and the possibility of causal powers operating on a variety of scales.

In Section 4, I argued that hylomorphism introduces an immanent, non-intentional form of teleology within nature, which makes sense of the normative and teleological aspects of the biological functions that individuate biological traits. In so doing, hylomorphism is able to affirm a real distinction between living organisms and heaps of matter, without recourse either to materialism or dualism, by affirming the teleological dimension within the identity conditions of biological systems. I explained why the normative aspect of biological function requires a constituent-based form of hylomorphism, in which substances of the same nature can be unified by their substantial forms to different degrees, in order to admit the possibility of malfunction in biological organisms where certain subsystems fail to perform their proper function. Finally, I deflated two common arguments against hylomorphism based on evolutionary science, and suggested that, rather than being incompatible with evolution, hylomorphism may have an explanatory role to play in the extended evolutionary synthesis.

References

Angier, T. (2021). *Natural Law Theory*. Cambridge University Press.

Austin, C. J. (2018). *Essence in the Age of Evolution: A New Theory of Natural Kinds*. Routledge.

Balme, D. M. (1987). Aristotle's Biology Was not Essentialist. In A. Gotthelf & J. G. Lennox (eds.), *Philosophical Issues in Aristotle's Biology* (pp. 291–312). Cambridge University Press.

Bedau, M. A. (1997). Weak Emergence. *Synthese, 31*, 375–99.

Bell, J. S. (1987). *Speakable and Unspeakable in Quantum Mechanics*. Cambridge University Press.

Bigelow, J., & Pargetter, R. (1987). Functions. *The Journal of Philosophy, 84*(4), 181–96.

Bishop, R. C., & Ellis, G. F. R. (2020). Contextual Emergence of Physical Properties. *Foundations of Physics, 19*(4047), 1–30.

Bohm, D. (1951). *Quantum Theory*. Prentice-Hall.

Bohm, D. (1952). A Suggested Interpretation of the Quantum Theory in Terms of 'Hidden' Variables. I. *Physical Review, 85*(2), 166–79.

Boulter, S. (2021). Evolution and the Principle of Proportionality. In *Neo-aristotelian Metaphysics and the Theology of Nature* (pp. 125–48). Routledge.

Boyle, R. (2000). *The Works of Robert Boyle, Vol. 10: Notion of Nature and other Publications of 1684–6* (M. Hunter & E. B. Davis, eds.). Pickering & Chatto.

Brower, J. E. (2017). Aquinas on the Individuation of Substances. In *Oxford Studies in Medieval Philosophy Volume 5* (pp. 122–50). Oxford University Press.

Button, T. (2013). *The Limits of Realism*. Oxford University Press.

Cartwright, N. (1999). *The Dappled World*. Cambridge University Press.

Chalmers, D. (1996). *The Conscious Mind: In Search of a Fundamental Theory*. Oxford University Press.

Cummins, R. (1976). Functional Analysis. *The Journal of Philosophy, 72*(20), 741–65.

de Broglie, L. (1928). La nouvelle dynamique des quanta [The new dynamics of quanta] *Electrons et photons. Rapports et discussions du cinquième Conseil de physique tenu à Bruxelles du 24 au 29 octobre 1927 sous les auspices de l'Institut international de physique Solvay*. Paris: Gauthier-Villars. pp. 105–32. English translation. In G. Bacciagaluppi &

A. Valentini (eds.), *Quantum Theory at the Crossroads: Reconsidering the 1927 Solvay Conference* (pp. 341–71). Cambridge University Press.

De Haan, D. D. (2017). Hylomorphism and the New Mechanist Philosophy in Biology, Neuroscience, and Psychology. In W. M. R. Simpson, R. C. Koons, & N. J. Teh (eds.), *Neo-Aristotelian Perspectives on Contemporary Science* (pp. 293–326). Routledge.

Dong, C.- H., Yang, L., Imoto, N. et al. (2008). Quantum Nondemolition Measurement of Photon Number via Optical Kerr Effect in an Ultra-high-Q Microtoroid Cavity. *Optics Express*, *16*(26), 21462–75.

Dorr, C. (2011). Physical Geometry and Fundamental Metaphysics. *Proceedings of the Aristotelian Society*, *111*(1pt1), 135–59.

Drossel, B., & Ellis, G. (2018). Contextual Wavefunction Collapse: An Integrated Theory of Quantum Measurement. *New Journal of Physics*, *20*(11), 113025.

Dumsday, T. (2012). A New Argument for Intrinsic Biological Essentialism. *Synthese*, *62*(248), 486–504.

Dumsday, T. (2016). Non-mereological Pluralistic Supersubstantivalism: An Alternative Perspective on the Matter/Spacetime Relationship. *Canadian Journal of Philosophy*, *46*(2), 183–203.

Eldredge, N., & Gould, S. J. (1989). APPENDIX: Punctuated Equilibria: An Alternative to Phyletic Gradualism. In *Time Frames* (pp. 193–224). Princeton University Press.

Ellis, G. F. R. (2021). Physics, Determinism, and the Brain. In J. Voosholz, M. Gabriel (eds.), *Top-Down Causation and Emergence* (pp. 157–214). Springer, Synthese Library.

Evnine, S. J. (2016). *Making Objects and Events: A Hylomorphic Theory of Artifacts, Actions, and Organisms*. Oxford University Press.

Fine, K. (1999). Things and Their Parts. *Midwest Studies in Philosophy*, *23*(1), 61–74.

Fine, K. (2012). Guide to ground. In F. Correia & B. Schnieder (eds.), *Metaphysical Grounding: Understanding the Structure of Reality*. Cambridge University Press.

Frankfurt, H. G. (1969). Alternate Possibilities and Moral Responsibility. *The Journal of Philosophy*, *66*(23), 829.

Funkestein, A. (1986). *Theology and the Scientific Imagination*. Princeton University Press.

Ghirardi, G. C., Rimini, A., & Weber, T. (1986). Unified Dynamics for Microscopic and Macroscopic Systems. *Physical Review D*, *34*(2), 470–91.

Gillespie, M. A. (2008). *The Theological Origins of Modernity*. University of Chicago Press.

Gillett, C. (2016). *Reduction and Emergence in Science and Philosophy*. Cambridge University Press.

Gregory, B. S. (2015). *The Unintended Reformation: How a Religious Revolution Secularized Society*. Harvard University Press.

Harré, R., & Madden, E. H. (1973). Natural Powers and Powerful Natures. *Philosophy, 48*(185), 209–30.

Heil, J. (2012). *The Universe As We Find It*. Oxford University Press.

Jaworski, W. (2011). *Philosophy of Mind: A Comprehensive Introduction*. John Wiley & Sons.

Jaworski, W. (2016). *Structure and the Metaphysics of Mind*. Oxford University Press.

Johnston, M. (2006). Hylomorphism. *The Journal of Philosophy, 103*(12), 652–98.

Kim, J. (1999). Making Sense of Emergence. *Synthese, 95*(1/2), 3–36.

Koons, R. C. (2014). Staunch vs. Faint-hearted Hylomorphism: Toward an Aristotelian Account of Composition. *Res Philosophica, 91*(2), 151–77.

Koons, R. C. (2018). Against Emergent Individualism. In *The Blackwell Companion to Substance Dualism* (pp. 377–93). John Wiley & Sons.

Koons, R. C. (2019). Thermal Substances: A Neo-Aristotelian Ontology of the Quantum World. *Synthese, 4*(2), 1–22.

Koons, R. C. (2021a). Design and Teleology: An Aristotelian-Thomistic Account of Life. *Unpublished Manuscript*. https://robkoons.net/work-in-progress.html.

Koons, R. C. (2021b). Essential Thermochemical and Biological Powers. In W. M. R. Simpson, R. C. Koons, & J. Orr (eds.), *Neo-Aristotelian Metaphysics and the Theology of Nature*. Routledge.

Koons, R. C. (2022). Sorting Out Aristotle. *Unpublished Manuscript*. https://robkoons.net/work-in-progress.html.

Koons, R. C., & Bealer, G. (eds.). (2010). *The Waning of Materialism*. Oxford University Press.

Koons, R. C., & Pruss, A. R. (2017). Must Functionalists Be Aristotelians? In J. D. Jacobs (ed.), *Causal Powers* (pp. 194–204). Oxford University Press.

Koslicki, K. (2008). *The Structure of Objects*. Oxford University Press.

Koslicki, K. (2018a). *Form, Matter, Substance*. Oxford University Press.

Koslicki, K. (2018b). Towards a Hylomorphic Solution to the Grounding Problem. *Royal Institute of Philosophy Supplement, 82*, 333–64.

Kripke, S. A. (1981). *Naming and Necessity*. Wiley-Blackwell.

Lagerlund, H., Hill, B., & Psillos, S. (eds.). (2021). *Reconsidering Causal Powers: Historical and Conceptual Perspectives*. Oxford University Press.

Leggett, A. J. (1992). On the Nature of Research in Condensed-state Physics. *Foundations of Physics*, *22*(2), 221–33.

Lennox, J. G. (1987). Kinds, Forms of Kinds, and the More and the Less in Aristotle's Biology. In A. Gotthelf & J. G. Lennox (eds.), *Philosophical Issues in Aristotle's Biology* (pp. 339–59). Cambridge University Press.

Lewis, D. (1970). How to Define Theoretical Terms. *The Journal of Philosophy*, *67*(13), 427.

Lewis, D. (1972). Psychophysical and Theoretical Identifications . *Australasian Journal of Philosophy*, *50*(3), 249–58.

Lowe, E. J. (2012). A Neo-Aristotelian Substance Ontology: Neither Relational Nor Constituent. In T. E. Tahko (ed.), *Contemporary Aristotelian Metaphysics* (pp. 229–48). Cambridge University Press.

Marmodoro, A. (2013). Aristotle's Hylomorphism without Reconditioning. *Philosophical Inquiry*, *37*(1/2), 5–22.

Marmodoro, A. (2014). *Aristotle on Perceiving Objects*. Oxford University Press.

Marmodoro, A. (2017). Power Mereology: Structural Powers Versus Substantial Powers. In M. P. Paoletti & F. Orilia (eds.), *Philosophical and Scientific Perspectives on Downward Causation* (pp. 110–27). Routledge.

Marmodoro, A. (2018). Whole, but Not One. In J. Heil, A. Carruth, & S. Gibb (eds.), *Ontology, Modality, and Mind Themes from the Metaphysics of E. J. Lowe* (pp. 60–70). Oxford University Press.

Martin, C. B. (1994). Dispositions and Conditionals. *The Philosophical Quarterly*, *44*(174), 1–8.

Maudlin, T. (1995). Three Measurement Problems. *Topoi*, *14*(1), 7–15.

Menzies, P., & Price, H. (2008). Is Semantics in the Plan? In D. Braddon-Mitchell & R. Nola (eds.), *Conceptual Analysis and Philosophical Naturalism* (pp. 159–82). MIT Press.

Millikan, R. G. (1984). Direct Proper Functions. In *Language, Thought, and Other Biological Categories*. The MIT Press.

Millikan, R. G. (1989). In Defense of Proper Functions. *Philosophy of Science*, *56*(2), 288–302.

Molnar, G. (2006). *Powers: A Study in Metaphysics* (S. Mumford, ed.). Oxford University Press.

Morrison, M. (2000). *Unifying Scientific Theories: Physical Concepts and Mathematical Structures*. Cambridge University Press.

Mumford, S., & Anjum, R. L. (2011). *Getting Causes from Powers*. Oxford University Press.

Nanay, B. (2010). A Modal Theory of Function. *The Journal of Philosophy*, *107*(8), 412 – 31.

Neander, K. (1991a). Functions as Selected Effects: The Conceptual Analyst's Defense. *Philosophy of Science*, *58*(2), 168–84.

Neander, K. (1991b). The Teleological Notion of 'Function'. *Australasian Journal of Philosophy*, *69*(4).

Nicholson, D. J., & Dupré, J. (2018). *Everything Flows: Towards a Processual Philosophy of Biology* (pp. 454–468). Oxford University Press.

Oderberg, D. S. (2007). *Real Essentialism*. Routledge.

Olson, R. G. (2004). *Science and Religion: 1450–1900*. The John Hopkins Press.

Omnès, R. (1994). *The Interpretation of Quantum Mechanics*. Princeton: Princeton University Press.

Owen, M. (2021). *Measuring the Immeasurable Mind: Where Contemporary Neuroscience Meets the Aristotelian Tradition*. Lexington Books.

Pasnau, R. (2011). *Metaphysical Themes 1274–1671*. Oxford University Press.

Pellegrin, P. (1987). Logical Difference and Biological Difference: The Unity of Aristotle's Thought. In A. Gotthelf & J. G. Lennox (eds.), *Philosophical Issues in Aristotle's Biology* (pp. 313–38). Cambridge University Press.

Peterson, A. S. (2018). Unity, Plurality, and Hylomorphic Composition in Aristotle's Metaphysics. *Australasian Journal of Philosophy*, *96*(1), 1–13.

Quarfood, M. (2006). Kant on Biological Teleology: Towards a Two-level Interpretation. *Studies in History and Philosophy of Science Part C: Studies in History and Philosophy of Biological and Biomedical Sciences*, *37*(4), 735–47.

Quine, W. V. (1960). *Word and Object*. MIT Press.

Reichenbach, H. (1956). *The Direction of Time*. Dover Publications.

Robinson, H. (2014). Modern Hylomorphism and the Reality and Causal Power of Structure: A Sceptical Investigation. *Res Philosophica*, *91*(2), 203–14.

Robinson, H. (2016). *From the Knowledge Argument to Mental Substance: Resurrecting the Mind*. Cambridge University Press.

Ruetsche, L. (2011). *Interpreting Quantum Theories*. Oxford University Press.

Schaffer, J. (2009). On What Grounds What. In D. Manley, D. J. Chalmers, & R. Wasserman (eds.), *Metametaphysics New Essays on the Foundations of Ontology* (pp. 347–83). Oxford University Press.

Schaffer, J. (2010). Monism: The Priority of the Whole. *Philosophical Review*, *119*(1), 31–76.

Schlosshauer, M. (2005). Decoherence, the Measurement Problem, and Interpretations of Quantum Mechanics. *Reviews of Modern Physics*, *76*(4), 1267–305.

Sellars, W. (1997). *Empiricism and the Philosophy of Mind*. Harvard University Press.

Silva, I. (2019). From Extrinsic Design to Intrinsic Teleology. *European Journal of Science and Theology*, *15*(3), 61–78.

Simpson, W. M. R. (2015). Comments on 'Hylomorphism, Powers and Perception', Delivered at the 'The Powers, Perception & Agency Conference' in Rome. *Unpublished Manuscript*. Oxford University Press.

Simpson, W. M. R. (2018). Knowing Nature: Beyond Reduction and Emergence. In A. B. Torrance & T. H. McCall (eds.), *Knowing creation* (pp. 237–260). Zondervan.

Simpson, W. M. R. (2020). *What's the Matter? Toward a Neo-Aristotelian Ontology of Nature* (Unpublished Doctoral Dissertation). Peterhouse, Cambridge University Press.

Simpson, W. M. R. (2021a). Cosmic Hylomorphism. *European Journal for Philosophy of Science*, *11*(28). https://link.springer.com/article/10.1007/s13194-020-00342-5.

Simpson, W. M. R. (2021b). From Quantum Physics to Classical Metaphysics. In W. M. R. Simpson, R. C. Koons, & J. Orr (eds.), *Neo-Aristotelian Metaphysics and the Theology of Nature* (pp. 21–65). Routledge.

Simpson, W. M. R. (2022). The Myth of the Physical Given. *Revue philosophique de Louvain*, *119*(1), 151–64.

Simpson, W. M. R. (2023). Small Worlds with Cosmic Powers. *The Journal of Philosophy*. Forthcoming.

Simpson, W. M. R., Koons, R. C., & Teh, N. J. (eds.). (2017). *Neo-Aristotelian Perspectives on Contemporary Science*. Routledge.

Simpson, W. M. R., Koons, R. C., & Orr, J. (eds.). (2021). *Neo-Aristotelian Metaphysics and the Theology of Nature*. Routledge.

Simpson, W. M. R., & Horsley, S. A. R. (2022). Toppling the Pyramids. In A. Marmodoro, C. Austin, & A. Roselli (eds.), *Time, Powers and Free Will* (pp. 17–50). Springer, Synthese Library.

Sober, E. (1980). Evolution, Population Thinking, and Essentialism. *Philosophy of Science*, *47*(3), 350–83.

Tabaczek, M. (2019). *Emergence: Towards a New Metaphysics and Philosophy of Science*. University of Notre Dame Press.

Tabaczek, M. (2023) *Theistic Evolution: A Contemporary Aristotelian-Thomistic Perspective*. Cambridge University Press.

Thompson, M. (2008). *Life and Action*. Harvard University Press.

Toepfer, G. (2008). Teleology in Natural Organized Systems and in Artefacts. In L. Illetterati & F. Michelini (eds.), *Purposiveness* (pp. 163–81). De Gruyter.

Toepfer, G. (2012). Teleology and Its Constitutive Role for Biology as the Science of Organized Systems in Nature. *Studies in History and Philosophy of Science Part C: Studies in History and Philosophy of Biological and Biomedical Sciences, 43*(1), 113–19.

van Inwagen, P. (1995). *Material Beings*. Cornell University Press.

Vemulapalli, G. K., & Byerly, H. (1999). Remnants of Reductionism. *Foundations of Chemistry, 1*(1), 17–41.

Walsh, D. M. (2020). Evolutionary Essentialism. *The British Journal for the Philosophy of Science, 57*(2), 425–448.

Walsh, D. M., & Wiebe, K. (2020). The Being of Living Beings. In A. S. Meincke & J. Dupré (eds.), *Biological Identity* (pp. 107–27). Routledge.

Ward, T. (2020). *Divine Ideas*. Cambridge: Cambridge University Press.

West-Eberhard, M. J. (2003). *Developmental Plasticity and Evolution*. Oxford University Press.

Williams, B. (2006). Hylomorphism. In M. Burnyeat (ed.), *The Sense of the Past* (pp. 218–28). Princeton University Press.

Wilson, J. (2015). Metaphysical Emergence: Weak and Strong. In T. Bigaj & C. Wüthrich (eds.), *Metaphysics in Contemporary Physics* (pp. 251–306). Brill.

Wilson, J. M. (2021). *Metaphysical Emergence*. Oxford University Press.

Wippel, J. F. (2000). *The Metaphysical Thought of Thomas Aquinas*. Catholic University of America Press.

Wolter, A. B., & Bychkov, O. V. (2004). *John Duns Scotus: The Examined Report of the Paris Lecture: Reportatio 1-A, (2 vols)*. franciscanpublications.com.

Wright, L. (1973). Functions. *Philosophical Review, 82*(2), 139–68.

Wright, L. (1976). *Teleological Explanations*. University of California Press.

Young, J. Z. (1971). *An Introduction to the Study of Man*. Oxford University Press.

Zimmerman, D. W. (1997). Immanent Causations. *Philosophical Perspectives, 11*, 433–71.

Acknowledgements

The author would like to thank (in alphabetical order) Alexander Pruss, Anna Marmodoro, Chris Oldfield, Daniel De Haan, John Marenbon, John Pemberton, Kathrin Koslicki, Paul Rimmer, Peter Day-Milne, Mariusz Tabaczek, Matthew Ntiros, Matthew Owen, Robert Koons, and Seth Hart for their critical feedback on different versions of this manuscript and their helpful suggestions, as well as two anonymous reviewers of Cambridge University Press. The author would also like to acknowledge the financial support of The John Templeton Foundation (via the international project, 'God and the Book of Nature', Grant Id: 61507); Wolfson College, Cambridge (during his time as a Junior Research Fellow); the Foundation for Excellence in Higher Education; and the Issachar Fund. The author is grateful to the British School at Rome for their hospitality during the final stages of preparing this manuscript for publication, and to the Angelicum (the Pontifical University of Saint Thomas Aquinas) for hosting him as a Visiting Scholar.

Cambridge Elements ≡

Philosophy of Biology

Grant Ramsey
KU Leuven

Grant Ramsey is a BOFZAP research professor at the Institute of Philosophy, KU Leuven, Belgium. His work centers on philosophical problems at the foundation of evolutionary biology. He has been awarded the Popper Prize twice for his work in this area. He also publishes in the philosophy of animal behavior, human nature and the moral emotions. He runs the Ramsey Lab (theramseylab.org), a highly collaborative research group focused on issues in the philosophy of the life sciences.

Michael Ruse
Florida State University

Michael Ruse is the Lucyle T. Werkmeister Professor of Philosophy and the Director of the Program in the History and Philosophy of Science at Florida State University. He is Professor Emeritus at the University of Guelph, in Ontario, Canada. He is a former Guggenheim fellow and Gifford lecturer. He is the author or editor of over sixty books, most recently *Darwinism as Religion: What Literature Tells Us about Evolution; On Purpose; The Problem of War: Darwinism, Christianity, and their Battle to Understand Human Conflict; and A Meaning to Life.*

About the Series
This Cambridge Elements series provides concise and structured introductions to all of the central topics in the philosophy of biology. Contributors to the series are cutting-edge researchers who offer balanced, comprehensive coverage of multiple perspectives, while also developing new ideas and arguments from a unique viewpoint.

Cambridge Elements ⁼

Philosophy of Biology

Printed in Great Britain
by Amazon

39912706R00046